How to be a
PROPERTY
MILLIONAIRE

If you want to know how...

Buying a House
A step-by-step guide to buying your ideal home

How to Get on the Property Ladder
*The first-time buyer's guide to escaping the rent trap
and owning your own home*

Buying a Property in France
An insider guide to realising your dream

Buy to Let in Spain
How to invest in Spanish property for pleasure and profit

howtobooks

Send for a free copy of the latest catalogue to:

How To Books
3 Newtec Place, Magdalen Road,
Oxford OX4 1RE, United Kingdom
email: info@howtobooks.co.uk
http://www.howtobooks.co.uk

How to be a
PROPERTY
MILLIONAIRE

FROM CORONATION STREET TO CANARY WHARF

ANNIE HULLEY

Her self-help guide to property investment

howtobooks

Published by How To Books Ltd,
3 Newtec Place, Magdalen Road,
Oxford OX4 1RE. United Kingdom.
Tel: (01865) 793806. Fax: (01865) 248780.
email: info@howtobooks.co.uk
http://www.howtobooks.co.uk

First edition 2004
Reprinted 2005

British Library Cataloguing in Publication Data
A catalogue record for this book is available from the British Library

Cover design by Baseline Arts Ltd, Oxford
Produced for How To Books by Deer Park Productions, Tavistock, Devon
Typeset by PDQ Typesetting, Newcastle-under-Lyme, Staffs.
Printed and bound by Bell & Bain Ltd, Glasgow

NOTE: The material contained in this book is set out in good faith for general guidance and no liability
can be accepted for loss or expense incurred as a result of relying in particular circumstances on
statements made in the book. The laws and regulations are complex and liable to change, and readers
should check the current position with the relevant authorities before making personal arrangements.

Contents

Preface

I was brought up in the North of England and my parents dabbled in the property market, so I can only assume that my interest in property must have been passed on from them. My parents were always happy to look around the odd property or two and as a child I found this house hunting preoccupation the most boring thing on earth. As an adult, however, I find property interesting, exciting and above all rewarding. My interest in bricks and mortar is not only a financial one, although as a property investor, this is and has to be the main consideration, but it is also of interest because of the challenge it offers in finding the right property, in the right place, for the right price.

As a student of the Bristol Old Vic Theatre School, I lived in rented accommodation for two years and like most students earned very little money, lived sparingly off a grant and eked out an existence. It was great fun but financially it was draining and although I would have loved to buy a bijou flat in Bristol, this simply was not an option. Like most students at that time and way before the concept of 'buy to let', renting was the only option.

When I finally moved to London in my early twenties with a suitcase, youthful optimism and an empty purse in hand, I had no choice but to rent again and this continued for several years until I could save enough to get on the property ladder. I bought my first flat when I was 27 and it was most certainly the best investment I have ever made because it gave me a start, a basis on which to build a property portfolio.

The great thing about my first flat was that it needed work doing to it but was perfectly liveable in at the same time. It was close to a tube station, which was my main priority, and it had a shared garden. After paying out for the mortgage and other costs, there was no money left in my budget to do any refurbishment work to the flat but each time I secured a job and had some surplus cash, I would invest the money in home improvements.

I was fortunate to know a good builder who became a friend and together, over time and on a limited budget, he helped me turn a run-down one bedroom apartment into a desirable property. I decorated it throughout, put in a new kitchen, lowered the ceilings to put in sound insulation and eventually sold it for a handsome profit. I was not only on the ladder but had moved off my first rung!

I have always been drawn to properties that need refurbishment and my next property was no exception. I had recently married and my husband and I both had capital to invest in a property. With our pooled resources we were able to purchase a three-bedroom, un-modernised house in a nice area. Location is always an important issue for me and I would rather buy a less grand house in a good area than a palace in a poor one.

Daunting though it can be to walk into a house that hasn't moved on in time at all, it is a great canvas from which to start to create your picture of your dream home. The most important aspect to consider before undertaking any large renovation project is to make sure you have enough money in the kitty to cover not only expected expenses but also to have a contingency budget if things go wrong. What I enjoyed about renovating this house was that it didn't have to be done all at once (it couldn't for financial reasons) but it still had all the original features and really just needed a plan to upgrade it and extend it. We knocked old walls down, put new walls in, replaced the kitchen and bathroom, built a loft conversion and even built a small out-building in the garden which housed our office. This office later became a unique selling point and when we finally put the house on the market after lovingly restoring it for several years it made us a considerable profit and was sold within a week. The message here is that if you are going to do any renovation, then do it right.

The next house, which is the one I currently live in, has been a huge project and is still on-going ... in fact it is never ending, but it was because of this investment fuelled by previous investments that we were able to re-mortgage and begin the serious business of building a property portfolio.

I now have a substantial investment property portfolio and that is the reason for writing this book, to show you that from humble beginnings, you too can achieve your goal of becoming a property millionaire!

Annie Hulley

Acknowledgements

The author gratefully acknowledges the help of the following people: Chris Clough for advice on tax and finance and also for the cover photograph; Martin Ogden of Horizon Mortgages; my solicitor Frank O'Neill; Fairhaven Holiday Cottages for information on holiday lets; Joy and Ray Cox for their hospitality and information on Spain; Ballymore Properties for giving me permission to be photographed outside New Providence Wharf and Alex Lawrie of ttapublications for information on Dubai.

I would like to dedicate this book to Chris, Jack and Lizzie

Getting On the Property Ladder

There is no easy answer to the problem of how to get on the property ladder, and rising levels of student debt can only mean young people will be forced to delay even longer getting their foot on the first rung. Currently the average age of a first-time buyer is 27 but is likely to rise to 30 over the next few years. If you are serious about becoming a property investor and making your million then get on the property ladder you must and as soon as possible. This chapter intends to explore ways in which you can take that first step.

MORTGAGES

The Council of Mortgage Lenders believes banks and building societies will have to adapt their mortgages to encourage first-time buyers into the property market. This could involve introducing shared mortgages or mortgages where the loan is guaranteed by a parent or guardian. A useful website to compare mortgages can be found at www.thisismoney.co.uk.

Guaranteeing the loan

The traditional loan from a mortgage company is three-and-a-half times the applicant's annual salary and this has presented a problem for first-time buyers. Some mortgage companies will now offer more than this, as long as a parent guarantees to cover repayments. Other mortgage companies only ask parents to cover the extra amount their child is borrowing above the normal three-and-a-half times salary.

Parents' income

Another scheme offered by some banks includes the parents' income when calculating what amount can be offered as a loan. This means that parents can purchase the property together with their child, although the parents' name will not be on the title deed to the property. This enables the child to borrow four times the highest wage, be it either theirs or their parents'.

Helping with the deposit

Some parents are re-mortgaging their house in order to use the capital raised to help their offspring with a deposit. If the parents re-mortgage carefully, their monthly payments may not rise that much and in some cases, if they get a better deal, the repayments may actually fall!

Using savings

Schemes are available from some building societies in which parents do not earn any interest on the money they pay into their offset account. Instead this interest is deducted from the value of their child's mortgage, before interest is calculated.

JOINING FORCES

If siblings or friends decide to buy together, it does not necessarily mean that they will have to live together. One could live in the property whilst the other rents out their room in the property, to pay for the mortgage. This enables the mortgage to be calculated on two incomes. When the property is sold, the profits can be divided into equal shares and can be used to finance deposits on individual properties.

RENTING TO STUDENTS

Some parents are choosing to buy a student home for their child.

They take out a buy to let mortgage and rent the student home to their offspring and other students, in order to cover the repayments. At the end of the student's university career, the house can be sold and any profits can be used to finance another deposit.

Deed of Gift

If parents buy a property for a child and their names are on the deed, they will have to pay capital gains tax when that property is sold. It is more tax efficient for students to raise a mortgage using their own names, in one of the ways explained above. Equally gifts of cash may be subject to inheritance tax, if the parent donor dies within seven years of the gift being made.

SHARED OWNERSHIP

Shared ownership means that you buy a share of a property, with a housing association owning the remaining share. You pay rent on the share that you don't own. Some housing associations specialise in low cost shared ownership and can offer properties for sale at as low a price as 30% of their market value. It is worth ringing your local housing association to see if it is involved in any shared ownership schemes. If it does operate such schemes, ask what criteria need to be met for you to be eligible to participate in the scheme.

If I participate in a shared ownership scheme, whom do I pay rent to?

You will pay rent to a registered social landlord. These are non-profit making organisations that provide and manage homes for rent or sale for people in housing need who cannot afford to buy. These landlords can be housing associations, housing societies or housing companies. These organisations are publicly funded by the local authority and by the Housing Corporation and operate nationwide. In some cases the social landlord can provide housing using their own money.

What is the Housing Corporation responsible for?

The Housing Corporation was set up by the government in 1964 to fund building projects by registered social landlords and to make sure that the homes built are of a certain standard. If a social landlord is not registered with the Housing Corporation then it will not receive any funding. The Housing Corporation also provides a monitoring service to ensure that social landlords maintain good standards of service on property management.

Who is eligible to participate in a shared ownership scheme?

- People in housing need, who cannot afford to purchase a home outright.
- Existing public sector tenants.
- People on social housing waiting lists.

Can I buy a shared ownership home with someone else?

Up to four people can become joint owners of a property but each individual must meet the criteria for eligibility.

What type of property is available on a shared ownership scheme?

Properties available can be anything from terraced houses to flats. They can be new or refurbished. These properties will generally be priced at the lower end of the market, so that they are within the financial means of applicants wishing to purchase under the shared ownership scheme.

How much of a share will I have to purchase?

This will depend on your own personal circumstances and how much you can afford, based on your income and savings. Most applicants buy a 50% share but this is by no means set in stone. You can purchase a 25% share to start with, or 75%, if your finances will allow. The higher the share you purchase, the less rent you will have to pay. You can increase your purchase share according to your financial situation at any time.

Where will I get the money to purchase a share?

You will have to apply to a mortgage company and the usual terms and conditions will apply, namely that your home will be at risk if you cannot meet your mortgage repayments. You will normally be eligible for tax relief on the first £30,000 of any mortgage and your repayments will vary as interest rates change.

> ### TIP
>
> Be sure to remember that if purchasing a flat, you will be required to pay any service charge on top of the mortgage and the rent.

Will I get a lease under shared ownership?

Whether you buy a house or a flat, the social landlord will grant you a lease for a standard term of 99 years. It will entitle you to live in your home as an owner-occupier and to buy further shares, if and when you choose. It will also allow you to sell your property, should you so wish. The lease will also cover your responsibilities regarding the repair and maintenance of the property. Although you have not bought the property in full, you will still have the same legal rights and responsibilities as any owner-occupier.

TIP

It is always advisable to seek legal advice on the terms and conditions of the lease.

How much rent will I have to pay?

The monthly rent will be a proportion of the total rent the property would fetch, calculated by the social landlord based on the proportion of the share you do not own. If you own 50% of the property you will be responsible for 50% of the rent. This rent will take into account the repayments you make as an owner-occupier and your share of any insurance, maintenance and repairs. This will work out less than if you were renting the whole property.

Will the rent stay the same?

The rent will be reviewed every year. Further share purchases by you will immediately become effective in reducing the rent.

Are there likely to be any other expenses that I should factor in when purchasing my share?

Stamp duty may be payable and you will need to check whether this duty will be applicable to your purchase. Some properties are exempt from stamp duty, for example those built in 'deprived areas' such as on 'brown field sites'. Stamp duty is also not levied on properties with a market value of less than £60,000. If stamp duty is payable you can either pay the duty on your share of the property only, or on the full value of the property. Your solicitor or legal advisor should be able to advise you on which option to take.

Repairs, insurance and service charges

If your home is a house, you will be responsible for all repairs and redecoration, both internally and externally. The social landlord will insure the structure of your home and you will have to pay a small management charge to cover this. If your home is a flat, you will be responsible for all internal repairs and redecoration. The social landlord will undertake to keep the building in which your flat is situated in good structural repair, to keep the structure insured and to keep any common parts decorated, cleaned and lit. You will have to pay a share of these costs, which will make up the service charge. The landlord will be accountable to you for any service charge spent and must consult you and provide you with estimates before any major work can take place. It will be your responsibility to contact your social landlord should any damage or defect occur.

I am interested in buying a shared ownership property, what is the procedure?

◆ Ask the social landlord for an application form.

◆ If you are suitable they will ask to meet you in person, to ascertain your requirements in full.

◆ If your requirements can be met, they will arrange for you to view a property.

◆ The price of such properties is usually based on an independent valuation.

◆ If you want to go ahead and buy, you agree what size share you would like to purchase and then apply for a mortgage.

◆ In some cases the social landlord may be able to advise you as to whom to contact about a mortgage. They will certainly know which banks and building societies are sympathetic to the scheme.

- If you save with a bank or building society, you can approach them with your requirements.

- If the lender needs to see a copy of the lease before agreeing any funds, ask the social landlord to send them a copy.

- Once your mortgage application has been successful and you have instructed a legal advisor, get in touch with the social landlord with this information.

- Your landlord will send a copy of the lease to your legal advisor, who will advise you on its contents.

- Your legal advisor will arrange a local search and investigate title to the property.

- You will be advised on the amount of rent and service charge that you will have to pay.

- Your purchase can then be formally completed and the property will be yours.

TIP

Ask your solicitor or legal advisor to check the lease, to see if any clause exists that will restrict you in the future as to whom you are allowed to sell your property to. Also ask them to check whether any restrictions apply that would prevent you buying further shares. These restrictions can sometimes apply, particularly in rural areas, where it is the social landlord's responsibility to keep a reasonable supply of low cost housing.

What is the procedure if I want to buy further shares in my home?

If you wish to purchase further shares in your property you will have to put this request in writing to your landlord, advising them of how big a share you wish to purchase. Your landlord will agree to have the property valued and will let you know the cost of your further share. You will have to pay for the valuation and you should be given three months to complete the mortgage and purchase your further share.

TIP

Remember that each time you purchase any further shares in your property you will be liable for the valuation fee. Make the most out of any further purchase of shares in your property by pushing yourself to the maximum you can afford, in order to avoid having to pay this recurring cost.

Can I make any alterations to my property?

If you wish to improve your home or make any structural alterations you will have to seek the landlord's written permission.

What happens when I want to sell my share of the property?

You may sell your property at any time but will have to advise the social landlord of your intention to move. You can either sell the part share you own or buy the remaining share, so that you can sell the property outright. You will of course benefit from any increase in value the property may have achieved. The downside of this is that the housing market can fall, as well as rise, so you need to consider the state of the market before you decide to sell.

TIP

Unless you absolutely have to, never ever sell in a falling market. Hang on in there if you can and wait for the market to rise again ... it generally does!

Can I sell to a private buyer?

Unless you own the property outright, clauses in the lease may enable the social landlord to nominate prospective buyers and to restrict the sale price with regards to an independent valuation report. The reason for this is that they wish the property to remain available to the people for whom shared ownership was intended.

Is there only one kind of shared ownership?

Some social landlords offer non-government-funded shared ownership schemes that work on the same principles but where the details can vary. Private developers can offer shared ownership schemes, where a wide range of similar conditions apply.

TIP

The demand for shared ownership homes is high, especially in areas where there are relatively few houses available. If you are accepted by a social landlord as a suitable candidate, you may have to wait some time for a suitable property to come along. However, turn this negative into a positive and start to save so that you can buy a bigger share of a property when one finally does come along.

Contact details for the Housing Corporation

Southeast

Croydon: Leon House, High Street, Croydon, Surrey CR9 1UH.
    Tel: 020 8253 1400. Fax: 020 8253 1444.
    Email: southeast.info@housingcorp.gsx.gov.uk

Southwest

Beaufort House, 51 New North Road, Exeter, EX4 4EP. Tel: 01392
    428200. Fax: 01392 428201.
    Email: southwest.info@housingcorp.gsx.gov.uk

East
Attenborough House, 109/119 Charles Street, Leicester LE1 1FQ.
　Tel: 0116 242. 4800 Fax: 0116 242 4801.
　Email: east.info@housingcorp.gsx.gov.uk

West Midlands
31 Waterloo Road, Wolverhampton VW1 4DJ. Tel: 01902 795000.
　Fax: 01902 795001.
　Email: westmidlands.info@housingcorp.gsx.gov.uk

Northeast
1 Park Lane, Leeds, LS3 1EP. Tel: 0845 230 7000. Fax: 0113 233
　7101. Email: northeastern.info@housingcorp.gsx.gov.uk

AFFORDABLE HOUSING
In London, developers who wish to build blocks of luxury flats
have to provide 25% affordable housing. This was a measure
brought in by Ken Livingstone to encourage key workers to stay
in the capital, rather than have them forced out because of high
property prices and steep rents. There are plans afoot for this
share to be increased to 50%, although this is being strongly
objected to by developers because it will narrow their profit
margins.

THE GOVERNMENT STARTER HOME INITIATIVE (SHI)
This was introduced to help key public sector workers, such as
teachers and nurses, buy their first home. The idea is to offer
equity loans to help plug the gap between mortgage allowances
and house prices. These were originally introduced with the
maximum equity loan available being £30,000, but this was later
increased to £50,000. Now there is a new scheme where some
public sector workers will qualify for loans of up to £100,000.

Contact your Local Government Housing Officer to find out what is available under the SHI or any similar schemes.

INCENTIVES

Many developers offer cash back schemes. The cash from these schemes can be put down as part of the deposit. Other developers offer deals which require only a 5% deposit.

SUMMARY

Anyone wishing to get on the property ladder will need to take advantage of any schemes offered that will enable them to do this. Remember your goal is to build a property portfolio and in order to do this you will need to lay foundations. A 25% share of a property is better than no share at all. So, if buying shares in a property is the only way you can get on to the ladder ... then do it and climb on!

2

Financing Your Purchases

This chapter will explain the simple formula of how, from a relatively small capital outlay, you can become a property millionaire. If you follow this advice you could have a very successful business that will provide you with full-time employment, a good income, an inflation-proof pension and a new career path.

RAISING MONEY

In the last few years there has been a huge growth in specialised mortgages for the property investor, including buy to let, second homes, self build and investing in properties abroad. It is now much easier to raise money, as many of these schemes are not solely related to the applicant's income. Self certification has freed the potential investor from relying on being able to borrow solely on multiples of declared earnings and can now take into account earnings from other areas – including letting income.

Opening doors to new investors

This has meant that all sorts of people who otherwise would not have had the credentials to raise money conventionally, can now legitimately do so and at an affordable price. This, in part, has been responsible for the huge increase in property investors. Other contributory factors are that property has outperformed the Stock Market over the last few years. Pensions have lost value and, more importantly, people want to take more personal responsibility for their own investments.

HOW TO GET ON THE PROPERTY PORTFOLIO LADDER

Obviously before you can buy your first investment property you need to have accumulated some capital – but not as much as you might think. The great thing about investing in property is that you don't have to fund the entire investment with your own money, as you would if you bought shares, for example. However, you will have to use some of your own money as the lender will require a deposit, but this can be as little as 15% of the purchase price.

TIP

In order to maximise your 'property profit potential' it is important that you use as little of your own nest egg as possible.

First steps

In order to be a successful property investor, you need a plan and some access to capital. This is not a 'get rich quick' scheme and has to be approached in a businesslike and professional manner. Cash flows must be prepared and emotion must be kept firmly in check.

HOW TO GET A NEST EGG

You must ask yourself how much capital you want to commit to this project and how you are going to raise it. Unless they have been left a sizeable inheritance, won the lottery or had an endowment policy mature, most people will not have a lump sum of capital at their disposal. However, if you already own your own property you may be able to re-mortgage and raise money on the increased value. Caution is needed, as you will need to meet the higher mortgage repayments, but in order to speculate, you have to accumulate and there is a certain degree of risk to all investments. This is certainly true of the property market but the trick is, as ever, to think it through and be prepared for the downside.

TIP

Flexibility is the key here. Don't tie yourself down to larger payments than you have to, as you can't predict the future.

WHEN SHOULD I SELL TO MAXIMISE PROFIT?

Although you can sell a property soon after you have renovated it or bought it off plan, the most effective way of investing in property is to hold on to it for at least five or ten years. If you do that then obviously the property should, at best, pay its own way or, at least, provide you with an operating profit. This is 'buy to let' and in order to do this there is a specific mortgage.

BUY TO LET MORTGAGES

Over the last five years there has been a revolution in the mortgage market which allows small investors to buy properties with products specifically designed for the small landlord. The big mortgage lenders have created specialised companies to deal with the explosion of interest in the buy to let market. This business is now worth £31 billion per year and as it is a very competitive market, there are good deals to be had. (See Chapter 4 for more on buy to let.)

What a mortgage lender needs

Unlike with a domestic mortgage, the amount that is being lent has nothing to do with the amount that you earn. The buy to let market has become a specialised business which works to different criteria than the domestic market. The lender is only interested in the rental potential of the property. On average that rental should be 130% of the annual interest payments.

Example
Property purchase price	£200,000
Deposit of 15%	£30,000
Loan from mortgage lender	£170,000

How to make the figures work

In order to get the full loan of £170,000 you will have to prove to the lender that the property will generate a gross annual income that covers the interest only payments, plus 30%. Most lenders will accept the previous owner's figures if there are any. If the property has not been rented out before, you will need to get a surveyor to estimate the rentals. The rental figure they are interested in is the gross amount before agent fees and any void periods. This criteria satisfies most lenders and actually works well, as it provides a good guide as to whether the property is a valid investment that will pay its way.

The all-important figure is what interest will be charged. For example, say you can get a loan at 5%.

Interest payments on loan are £170,000 × 5%	= £8,500 per year.
Gross rent needed (130% of £8,500)	= £11,050 per year.
The rental required is £11,050	= £921 per month.

If your rental figures are not high enough then you will have to use more of your own money, until the rent covers the interest payments.

GETTING THE RIGHT MORTGAGE

It really is worth shopping around for mortgages. Check the
adverts in the newspapers and on the Internet, as well as
information direct from the building societies and banks. This is
big business and there is a lot of competition so have a good look
around. You should also ask for some quotes from specialist
brokers.

Using a broker

A broker will make a charge, anything from a one off payment, or
0.5% to 1% of the loan. The advantage of using an independent
broker is that they are specialists and know where to find the best
rates.

There might be special deals only offered to brokers which you
wouldn't otherwise be eligible for. Or, if you put down a larger
deposit you might get a much better rate, which may persuade you
to part with more of your own precious capital.

Going it alone

If you don't want to use a broker you can still find a lot of good
mortgage deals but beware of the small print. A lot of loans have
penalty clauses which may catch you out, especially if you want to
sell the property or move to a better deal before the term has
expired. These can be quite hefty for example – 4% of the loan in
the first year, 3% in the second, 2% in the third and so on.
Brokers may get you a cheaper deal without the penalties but then
it will cost you money up front.

What is the role of the surveyor in getting a mortgage?

An additional advantage of using a large, well established broker is that they have good relationships with surveyors. This can play a very major part as everything is reliant on the surveyor's valuation. Some surveyors may not know the area well, may be very cautious or out of date with their valuations. You are not allowed to coerce or influence their valuations, as they are viewed as impartial by the lender. However, you do not want the wrong person valuing your property because the amount that you can borrow will be dependent on their figures. If the valuation is too low then you will be seriously out of pocket.

TIP

If you think the surveyor's figures are wrong, send a list of comparable property prices to the surveyor. I have done this before when a valuation did not add up and as a consequence the valuation was increased substantially. Remember you don't want to put down any more of your capital than you have to. The trick really is to use borrowed money – as you will see later.

WHAT TYPE OF MORTGAGE?

Most investors tend to take out an interest only mortgage because there is little point in making scheduled repayments. You don't want valuable cash flow going back unnecessarily to the lender, plus the repayment terms won't work to your advantage. Many mortgages allow capital repayments to be made during the course of the loan, so you can pay in lump sums if you want to.

To fix or not to fix?

This is a constant conundrum and you have to play your hunch when deciding whether to choose a fixed rate mortgage. Do you think rates will go up or down? If you think they will go up – how much will they go up? Inevitably fixed rates are higher than the variable rates and they will have penalties for early repayments. Fixed rates are dependent on what the Futures Market thinks might happen. If you fix and interest rates go down, you will be locked into that rate for the term of the loan and will have to pay hefty penalties if you want get out and change to a cheaper rate.

Variable rate mortgages

If you stay on the variable rate then you will win out if interest rates go down but if they go up then your profits will be eaten into. However, with variable rates there are plenty of deals around that do not have penalties – so you can jump into a fixed rate if you get worried. If you fix and the rates go up, then you will be happy in the knowledge that your property is not going to cost any more.

EXPANDING YOUR PROPERTY PORTFOLIO

The more properties that you purchase, the greater the profits you will make in a rising market. However, most people are on a limited budget, so the problem is, how do you expand your property portfolio?

Re-mortgaging

The answer is re-mortgaging. It works quite simply. What have you done with the first property that you bought for £200,000?

◆ Renovated it completely?

◆ Redecorated it, changed the colour scheme, carpets and curtains so it looks more up-market?

◆ You bought off plan two years ago, the property has just been completed and prices have now risen?

♦ You bought in an up-and-coming area. After renting out the property for a couple of years the area that you bought in has improved and the property prices have increased as a result?

As you are a property investor, you will have carried out one of these options and the value of the property will have increased. As a result you can raise more money on the property and free up some more of your precious capital to invest in another property.

How does this work?

Remember how a buy to let mortgage works? You have to put down a 15% deposit on the value of the property and prove to the lender that the gross rental income will cover the interest charge by 130%. Let's look at our property now. Two years on, it has been valued by the surveyor at £250,000.

Property valued at	£250,000
15% deposit	£37,500
Loan from mortgage lender	£212,500
Previously your loan was	£170,000
Profit to re-invest with	£42,500

Meeting the criteria

This is called gearing. You are re-investing paper profits on your property without having to sell it or pay tax on it. However, re-mortgaging is not just a theoretical exercise, the mortgage lenders are encouraging of the practice and, providing you meet the criteria, they will lend you the enhanced amount. You will, however, still have to achieve the rental figure of 130% of the annual loan interest rate. Which in this case is:

$$£212,500 \times 5\% = £10,625 \text{ per annum}$$
Or £885 per month $\times$ 130% = £1,151.

You have now made a paper profit of £42,500, which you can re-invest in another property and you haven't had to pay a penny in tax. Do you know a better way of making money?

WHY EXPAND YOUR PORTFOLIO?
There are several reasons for this. Primarily you will increase your 'property profit potential' at the same time as spreading your risks across a number of different properties that are successfully being rented out. The tenants are paying the mortgages, while the properties are increasing in value.

Example
With the £42,500 you buy two properties for £125,000 each. Let's do the sums as before:

2 new properties worth	£250,000
Deposit at 15%	£37,500
Mortgage loans	£212,500

All the criteria are met for the mortgage lender, both properties have been cosmetically improved and are soon tenanted.

Flash forward
It is now three years since you bought the two properties. Again you made wise choices and the value of the flats has increased. The average capital gain in property per annum over the last 20 years has been 6%. Recently there have been double digit increases, but remember prices can go down as well as up, so it is

always wise to be conservative in your estimates. However, if you have followed the guidelines in this book and bought the right properties in the right areas then these figures should look much more encouraging. But for the purposes of this exercise let us assume the value of each property has gone up by 20% over the three years.

Value of Property No. 1 was	£250,000	
20% rise over 3 years	£50,000	£300,000
Value of properties 2 & 3 was	£250,000	
20% rise over 3 years	£50,000	£300,000
Value of portfolio		£600,000
Outstanding loans to mortgage lender		£425,000
Your share of the value		£175,000
Initial deposit		£30,000
Profit		**£145,000**

Flashback

Now if you go back in time to when you bought your first property, you put up a deposit of £30,000. This is the only money you have invested in the portfolio. Everything else has been raised on the value of the properties, with the interest being paid by the tenants of those properties. This represents a profit figure of £145,000 or 482% over the period.

Rewards

It's a great way to make money. It required some input but it has not been full time, allowing you to continue your normal paid occupation. You will have had to study the market, make value judgements and take the risk but the rewards are plainly there to be taken.

The conservative approach
If you had not been so entrepreneurial but had stuck with the initial investment of the first property – then the figures would look like this:

Value of property at purchase	£200,000
Initial increase in value	£50,000
Second increase in value	£50,000
Present market value	£300,000
Loan from mortgage lender	£170,000
Your share in value	£130,000
Initial deposit	£30,000
Profit	**£100,000**

On your initial investment of £30,000 you have made a 330% profit. Not bad, but by purchasing two more properties at no extra cost to yourself, your profit would have leapt up from £100,000 to £145,000.

Spreading the risk
By buying more property you have made an extra £45,000. All the properties have increased in value so you can re-mortgage them and raise more investment cash to increase your portfolio and profit potential. By 'gearing up', you are also spreading your risk over more properties. Void periods and any maintenance charges will be spread out and the additional income will ease the pain.

Further expanding your portfolio
As your portfolio has increased in value, you decide to continue investing and buy another three properties at £200,000 each, making a total of £600,000.

Say another three years have passed and values have increased by another 20%.

Example

Initial portfolio	£600,000
3 recent properties	£600,000
Value of portfolio	£1,200,000
Increase in value by 20% over 3 years	£240,000
Value of portfolio	£1,440,000
Outstanding loans to mortgage lender	£935,000
Your share in value	**£505,000**

So eight years after making an initial investment of £30,000, you have become a property millionaire, as you own £1.4 million pounds of property, of which your share in that value is £505,000.

MANAGING THE PORTFOLIO

These figures are only examples but they do represent the formula for making money out of property investment. The interesting thing about this business is how quickly investors get the hang of it and how soon you overcome your initial fears of dealing with figures that look so large. On average, the number of properties owned by 'serious buy-to-let investors' is 11. It's not hard to see why. An individual – or better still, a couple – can manage 11 properties between them whilst keeping the day job – and the multiples work well at this level.

Caution

BUT BEWARE – don't get carried away with ploughing every spare penny into investing in new properties. Do not over-gear but keep an eye on your cash flow. If you can't pay your bills, you will be in trouble. It's not always easy to raise cash quickly by selling a property. You might have a tenant and if they are untidy, the property will not show well. With a tenant in place, your market is restricted to investors. The market might not be favourable and completing on a sale takes a long time. So don't convince yourself that you can get out of trouble at the last minute by selling a property. Selling a property takes time and planning.

TIP

It is vital to keep sufficient cash in hand to deal with unforeseen costs, such as rises in interest rates (if not on fixed rates), maintenance of properties and void periods.

SUMMARY

Initially the figures do look quite frightening and could lead to sleepless nights. But you can get used to dealing with these figures. You will relax more as you maximise the profit potential of the properties by renting them out successfully. Within a few years, you could have created a sizeable portfolio, which will not only provide an income but will also increase in capital value.

3

Buying at Auctions

Auctions can be a good way of investing in property. Although bargains are getting harder and harder to find these days, they are still out there if you are prepared to do your homework. If you are keen to make money out of property and achieve the maximum 'property profit potential', renovating a run-down property can still be your best bet and you can find these types of properties at auction. It is important, however, that you follow certain rules and stick to them, no matter what.

WHAT TYPE OF PROPERTY GOES UNDER THE HAMMER AT AUCTION?

The properties on offer at auction can range in price from £3,000 to £4m +. They can be flats, houses, residential or commercial. They can be barns, windmills, water towers, houseboats, lock ups, land and public conveniences! They can vary in how much work they will need. Some will only require a simple cosmetic job, whilst others can be a complete wreck needing total refurbishment.

WHO SELLS AT AUCTIONS?

Properties that sell at auction are generally those that you cannot buy through a traditional estate agent. Increasingly, properties are being off-loaded by councils and housing associations who are simply looking for the best price on the day. You will also find large houses that have been divided into bed-sits that could be turned back into single residences, or hotels that are long past their sell by date and in need of total refurbishment. Other properties can be probate sales, whilst others can have title problems. Basically, properties for sale at auction are those where a quick sale is desired, or where getting a mortgage would be difficult and in some cases impossible.

TIP

If you are thinking of converting a house from bed-sits into a single dwelling with a view to making it into a family home, either to live in or for re-sale, check whether other similar properties in the area are being converted. Is the property near to good schools? Get at least three quotes from local builders to find out how much the work will cost. Contact the local planning department to see if the property is in a conservation area and find out whether there are any covenants or planning restrictions which would prevent you from making the changes you would want.

WHO BUYS AT AUCTION?

Developers/builders who want to renovate a property and then sell it on for a quick profit. People who are interested in the challenge of doing up a property from scratch to live in, so that they can design it exactly how they want it, without having someone else's stamp on it. Buy to let investors and shrewd property investors.

HOW DO I GO ABOUT BUYING AT AUCTION?

First and foremost you must find out when, where and by whom the auction is going to be held and ask for their catalogue. Most property auctions will be advertised in property newspapers and some of the big agents run their own auctions, so it is worth making a few phone calls to established estate agents to find out what is in their calendar. Allsop & Co, the UK's largest property auctioneer, provide online catalogues at www.allsop.co.uk. It is also worth checking with local auction houses to see if they have anything coming up and you can also try the Royal Institute of Chartered Surveyors. Useful websites are:

www.propertyauctions.com

www.auctionpropertyfor-sale.co.uk

TIP

If you are thinking of buying at an auction, then attend a few first, as a spectator, rather than a purchaser. It is important that you get a feel for how things are done, as buying at auction can be quite a nerve-wracking experience even for the most seasoned professional. Once the adrenaline starts to pump (believe me it will) and you are serious about buying something at an auction, then you need to be in control. If you have visited a couple of auctions prior to purchasing at one, this will help you keep a sense of balance. Observe first ... then participate!

I've got the catalogue and am interested in a property, what do I do next?

You must do your detective work and unfortunately this will cost you money.

◆ It is essential that you view the properties which interest you as soon as possible. Viewing arrangements can be made through the auctioneer.

◆ Check the legal documentation. For each lot there will be special conditions of sale, plus other documentation provided by the vendor's solicitor. There may be a small charge to have this information sent to you.

◆ Instruct a solicitor to check that there are no problems with the title deeds or the purchase contract.

◆ Arrange to get a survey done. Ask your surveyor to do you a breakdown of likely repair costs.

◆ Arrange your finances. If the property is eligible for a mortgage, you will need to get a valuation done by a mortgage company.

TIP

A few days before the auction check with the auction team that any lots you are interested in are still available. Sometimes, frustratingly, they can be withdrawn!

What does the guide price actually mean?

The guide price is the catalogue price. Guide prices are often deliberately conservative and often bear little relation to what the property, realistically, should be able to achieve at auction. Auctioneers do this to stir up interest in the auction and it is fair to say that no one, not even the auctioneer, can predict how the bidding will go on the day.

What is the reserve price?

The reserve price is the lowest price the seller will accept. If a property does not reach the reserve price it will be withdrawn.

Is there a downside to buying at auction?

If the property represents the possibility of a real bargain, you can bet your bottom dollar that you will not be the only one interested in it. This could result in you paying out a lot of preparation costs, only to end up being outbid. It is important to remember when bidding that the valuation put on a property by the lender may be considerably below the final hammer price, leaving you with a shortfall to find.

Is there an upside to buying at auction?

You can get a bargain. It also is a straightforward buying process and means that once the auctioneer's gavel has fallen, you effectively own the property and cannot be gazumped.

TIP

If you have been bidding for a property that has been withdrawn, because it failed to reach its reserve price, and you are prepared to up your last bid, it may be worth your while speaking to the auctioneer after the sale, as the vendor may be prepared to accept an offer.

HOW TO BID

Raise your hand or catalogue clearly when bidding. Once you have decided on a price that you consider the property to be worth, do not exceed it. Tempting though it may be to go that little bit higher, do not get caught up in a bidding frenzy. This is where self control must be exercised and, although you may have had to spend money researching the property, it is far safer to chalk up a few hundred pounds loss, than to buy a property that is way out of your price range.

I HAVE SUCCESSFULLY BID FOR MY PROPERTY, WHAT HAPPENS NEXT?

You must sign the contract agreeing to purchase the property and pay 10% of the purchase price as a deposit, plus the auction administration fee. Effectively, what you are doing here is exchanging contracts, only at a much faster pace than the conventional way of purchasing a property. The next step is that you will have to complete on the agreed contract date. This is generally 28 days after you have signed the contract at the auction. It is important that all the legal documents are in place by the agreed contract date, otherwise you will be at risk of having to forfeit your deposit.

DO I HAVE TO BE PRESENT AT THE AUCTION IF I WANT TO BID FOR A PROPERTY?

There are several ways to bid at auction if you do not want to be there in person. This can be done in various ways:

- phone
- fax
- internet
- solicitor.

If you are going to choose any of these options, you must have filled in a registration form, prior to the auction. It will also be necessary to arrange funds to cover the anticipated deposit.

IS IT POSSIBLE TO PURCHASE A PROPERTY PRIOR TO THE AUCTION?

When a property is available to be sold prior to auction, the catalogue and any subsequent publicity will state 'unless previously sold'. This will mean that should you wish to purchase this property prior to the auction, you will have to complete the purchase procedure. Contracts will have to be signed and the deposit paid.

TIP

It is the auctioneer's job to ratchet up the price as much as they can. They will probably have several lots to auction and will want to keep the bidding brisk and in big denominations. Try to break down the bids. If the bidding is going up by a thousand pounds a time, try to slow it down by raising the bid by only five hundred pounds a time. Similarly, if the bidding is going up at £500 a time then put in bids raising it only £100 a time. Finally, when the bidding has slowed down considerably, up the bid significantly. This will change the momentum of the bidding and take those bidding against you by surprise. The golden rule remains the same, of course: do not go above your ceiling price!

IF YOU WANT TO SELL AT AUCTION

A property auctioneer who will be a member of the MRICS/ FRICS will advise you whether your property is suitable to sell at auction. Most properties that come up for sale at auction are ones that have something different about them, be it good or bad. Your average semi-detached or terraced house which needs no more than a cosmetic touch up would probably achieve a better price sold the conventional way, through an estate agent.

FINALLY

It is important to remember, before you snap up a bargain at auction, you need to have a good available work force behind you. Once you have successfully bid, the property is yours and you will have to pay for it. So the sooner you can get the property renovated, the better. Even if you are good at DIY and intend to do a lot of the work yourself, your skills alone may not be enough to turn that ugly duckling of a property into a swan. So, if it is your first project, don't be over ambitious, start off small and always have money left over in the budget for contingencies ... because you will probably need it!

SUMMARY

It is possible to get a bargain at auction, especially if you are looking for a renovation project. The important thing is to do your homework beforehand, decide on your upper limit and stick to it.

Buy to Let

As a property investor, 'buy to let' is the name of the game. Although I enjoy the rewards of the occasional 'flip' (which is to sell a property on before completion), the core of my property portfolio is buying properties to rent out. This increases my chances of maximising 'property profit potential', as any hiccups in the property market, such as price falls, should level out in the long term.

The principle of buy to let is that the investor purchases the property in order to enjoy long-term capital gains, while the tenant pays the mortgage. However, there are many factors to consider before plunging in and buying a property. This chapter will highlight some of those factors and concentrate on key issues: where to buy, what to buy and who to buy for.

It is also important to decide before choosing a buy to let property whether you are investing for yield, capital gain, or in an optimistic market – both!

THE BUY TO LET MARKET

The buy to let market has seen a large increase in the number of re-mortgaging applications. Investors understand the theory that house price increases coupled with rental income is an attractive proposition, compared with returns from pensions or other forms of investment. However, as expected, the rate of growth is now slowing. This trend is expected to continue over the next couple of years, so it is important, when choosing property as an investment, that you research the market thoroughly.

What is yield?

Your yield is basically your profit, a percentage of what you earn from renting out your buy to let property, after all the expenses of purchasing and the running costs are subtracted. For example:

£100.000 purchases an apartment.

A 10% rental income would be £10.000.

This would represent a 10% (gross) yield.

A simple formula for working out the yield

Weekly rent × 52 = annual rent.

Say the weekly rent is £150 × 52 = £7,800.

Subtract the agency fees. Agency fees of 10% = £780.

Deduct £780 from £7,800 = £7,020.

Subtract the property out-goings. Say property out-goings are £520.

Subtract £520 from £7,020 = £6,500.

Multiply the figure remaining by 100.

£6,500 × 100 = £650,000.

Divide that by the purchase price.

Say the purchase price is £100,000.

£650,000 divided by £100,000 = 6.5%.

What remains is the net return = 6.5%

Compare the net return to the current interest rate.

What are the property out-goings likely to be?

It is advisable to consider the points listed below when working out your profit margin, as these will affect your overall yield.

Voids

A void is when the property is not rented out. It would be prudent to include a six week void period when calculating the overall anticipated yield for the investment property.

Service charge/ground rent

You will be expected to pay the full service charge and ground rent, whether the property is occupied or not. Both these charges will have to be subtracted from your gross yield.

Set up costs

These will include furniture (should you chose to let the property furnished), stamp duty and legal fees.

Maintenance/repairs/redecoration

You, as the landlord, will be responsible for maintenance, repair and redecoration. You should estimate a 'what if things go wrong' budget, to cover any unexpected repairs, such as the boiler breaking down, for instance. It is always wise to have a contingency fund and you should subtract this from your 'gross' yield.

Insurance

This will be another expense to deduct from the 'gross' yield and you should budget for both contents and building insurance (if this is not included in a service charge).

Electricity and gas safety inspections

All rented accommodation is expected to have annual checks on its services. You will need to get safety certificates from a qualified electrician and a Corgi registered plumber, in respect of gas.

Cleaning
The property will have to be cleaned to a professional standard at the beginning of each tenancy.

Council tax
You will be responsible for 'empty rate' council tax, when the property is unoccupied.

Utility bills
During 'void' periods you will be responsible for all utility bills.

TIP

Purchase in the lower section of the market, as the returns are generally higher.

What is considered a good yield?
A good yield can range from 6% to 10%. I know of some investment landlords who would not touch a property without a minimum of a 10% yield but this is not always possible and depends on the area you invest in. If the local market is saturated, this will have a negative effect on your anticipated yield, as there will be a lot of competition to get tenants. Supply will outweigh demand, rents will be reduced and standards will have to be high, if you are to avoid voids.

Do your sums
Work out the return before you buy. In order to maximise your 'property profit potential', you need to base your decision on likely returns, and not on personal and emotional taste.

TIP

Make a list of all the expenses, including mortgage and other property related costs you anticipate, before you invest. If the profit margins are too tight and the rental does not net you enough income, then it is likely this property will not be the right investment for you – if your main objective is yield.

CHOOSING THE RIGHT PROPERTY

If you choose the right property, in the right area, you should be onto a winner. Make sure the property is in an area well suited to letting. Take advice from the local letting agents as to what types of property are in demand.

What type of person is looking to rent?

- Young singles
- Working professionals
- Groups of people wanting to share i.e. students
- Couples (married or otherwise)
- Families
- People on housing benefits
- Divorcees
- Professionals relocating
- Basically anyone!

WHAT TYPE OF PROPERTY SHOULD I BE LOOKING FOR?

This will depend on what type of tenant you are hoping to attract and where you are choosing to invest, be it city, town or country.

- **Studio flats**. Popular with students, as the rents required for these are often all they can afford. In inner city areas they can be used as a weekly base for a working professional whose principal home is out of town.

- **One bedroom flats**. This type of property offers the best rental possibilities in an inner city area. They are more popular with young professionals than studio flats. The one disadvantage of this type of property is that it often comes without parking.

- **Two bedroom apartments**. This type of property is popular with young couples or two people sharing. It is preferable for this type of property to have two bathrooms and parking.

- **Small terraced houses**. If they are located in a city they could appeal to couples or sharers. They could also appeal to a family with young children but would need to have a garden.

- **Large houses**. If situated near a university, this type of property would be ideal for student sharers. It could also be suitable as a family home, if it was situated close to schools and transport links.

TIP

A general rule of thumb is that apartments are the preferred rental properties in inner city areas, whereas houses are more suitable in small towns and rural locations. If you are in any doubt at all as to what property will be most suitable for letting in a given area, consult the professionals and read the local property papers.

Renting to young professionals

If you are aiming to rent out to young professionals, you will want a property close to office blocks, shops or industry. Young professionals are preferred by many buy to let investors, as they are generally in stable employment. Reference checks will indicate whether they are able to pay the rent, although this does not mean that they necessarily will. They also tend to make fewer demands on a property, as they will generally only be using it as a base.

However, such tenants are in great demand, so make sure the market isn't saturated with similar types of properties sitting void because of over-supply, before you decide to invest. A lot of young workers tend to rent in the month of September, which is partly due to starting work after the end of the academic year. January is also a busy time for rentals, as people often try to change their lifestyle at the start of a new year.

Key factors to attract young professionals
- Job opportunities in the area.
- Easy transport links.
- Restaurants/nightlife.
- Proximity to shops and food stores.
- Apartments with leisure facilities.
- Stripped wood floors.
- Neutral décor.
- Modern appliances.

TIP

I always put a microwave into my properties when I am renting to a young professional. I find the majority of young professionals are not keen on cooking, largely because they do not have the time. Supplying a microwave also saves a lot of wear and tear on the oven and hob.

Case study
I once rented out a brand new flat for a year to a young working man and at the end of the tenancy the packaging was still in the oven – it had never been used – although the microwave showed signs of the odd takeaway or two!

Corporate lets

These are the most desirable kind of lets, as you are actually renting your property out to a company, rather than an individual. There is, however, no guarantee that a company won't get into financial difficulties, but you are less likely to get a 'default' on rental payments than you are with an individual. Corporate lets can come through location agents, whose job is to find accommodation for company employees who are coming to work in the area. Their first port of call will be to the more established letting agents in the vicinity.

These lets can last from six months to three years and will generally have a pre-negotiated rental increase built in for each year, depending on the length of the tenancy! They can be the most hassle-free lets but you will probably have to agree to have the property professionally managed. Together with the 10% letting fee this can cost you anything up to 16% of the gross rent.

Key factors for corporate lets
- The property will have to be professionally managed.
- The property will need to be well presented.
- It should have a 'power' shower.
- Leisure facilities and 24-hour concierge will be an advantage.
- The property needs to be in the best location.
- Fixtures and fittings need to be of a high standard.
- The kitchen needs to be fully equipped with modern appliances.
- The property will need secure parking.

TIP

If a letting agent charges in excess of 16% for letting and full management, and they refuse to negotiate on commission – go to another agent!

Letting to students

If you are considering letting to students you will want an investment property close to the university or college. It is unlikely you will want an upmarket property for this type of let, as students have limited incomes and a lot to spend it on. Rent is not generally something they will want to spend too much on! A house with several rooms that can be let out to a group sharing is the best type of accommodation for this market. It may be a group of friends or a group of individuals, so expect parties.

TIP

Don't put any expensive furniture items in the property. Durable and practical is best, because it is very likely to take quite a hammering. Students, by their very nature, are not the most conservative of tenants.

Key points when letting to students

- It should be a large house (preferably four bedrooms) with proximity to a 'learning' centre.
- Durable furnishings.
- Preferably no garden.
- Good appliances and white goods.
- Heavy duty carpets in dark colours.
- Washable covers and curtains.
- Gas central heating (to avoid condensation problems).
- Outside space ... to park bicycles!

TIP

Make sure the plumbing is up to scratch, as the boiler, shower and washing machine will all suffer from heavy use! Make sure all appliances can stand up to wear and tear. It would be a false economy to buy cheap white goods, as you will end up having to replace them sooner rather than later.

What are the benefits of renting to students?
This type of accommodation can often be very good for yield, as the properties do not incur expensive service charges.

What are the disadvantages?
These properties can often be void during the summer months, after the academic year has ended. There will also be regulations, particularly regarding fire precautions, that will need to be adhered to when renting out a property to students or any multiple occupancy households. Consider these estimated costs when calculating the yield.

What defines a multiple occupancy household?
Under the Planning Act, 'multiple occupation' is quantified as eight or more unrelated people, living in a single dwelling unit, whether under a single tenancy agreement or as a number of tenancies, i.e. bed-sits. Under the Housing Act, it can also mean two or more unrelated people living in the same house, even if they are a couple! However, when the tenants are a couple and where there is no evidence of separation between the occupants, the regulations are not as stringent regarding fire safety issues. This is because the bedrooms are used, in principal, for sleeping and not for living in. In bed-sits, where a room is used for sleeping, living and cooking, the risk of fire is increased. Safety measures have to be put into place and are legally enforceable by your local authority.

What kind of safety measures will I need to put in place?
Your local authority will be able to offer you guidelines but basically you will need to consider installing:

♦ fire doors
♦ self closers on all doors

- integrated smoke and heat detectors
- emergency lighting
- fire escapes.

Will installing safety measures add value to the property?
These safety measures, can, of course, work out to be very expensive and there is no guarantee that you will recover these costs when you choose to sell, unless it is to another landlord. If you choose to sell to an owner-occupier, the safety measures you have been forced to comply with could actually devalue the property.

TIP

If you are considering buying a house that has already complied with 'Housing in Multiple Occupation' regulations, always negotiate on the actual market value of the property, not on the income it may generate. This will be an important consideration when you decide to sell, as your future buyer may be an owner-occupier.

Letting to housing benefit claimants
This type of tenant can be anyone from the unemployed, to the single mother, to someone who has just lost their job or been made redundant. It does not necessarily mean someone who is dishonest and it is worth remembering that anyone can fall on hard times, even property investors who don't do their research! If you want to rent to this type of tenant you would be advised to contact your local authority's Housing Benefit Department, as the rules about claiming this kind of benefit can be complicated and you will need to know what conditions apply.

Who will set the rent?

Should you decide to rent to this type of tenant you will be visited by a rent officer, who will inspect the property and inform you what rent the local authority is prepared to pay, taking into account the claimant's personal circumstances.

What are the disadvantages of this type of let?

If you have a two bedroom property and the Benefits Department consider the claimant needs only one bedroom, they will only agree to pay a proportion of the rent and it will be up to the tenant to cover the rest. If the tenant has no means of income, this could be a risky undertaking for a landlord.

Is the rent the local authority agrees to pay guaranteed?

Yes and no! The local authority will pay the rent that has been set but not necessarily directly to you or your agent. Even if the method of payment has been agreed between all the parties concerned, the tenant can change this arrangement whenever they wish to do so. The local authority will not inform the landlord of this change. If the tenant decides not to pay the landlord, then it is up to the landlord to chase the tenant for the arrears. If this results in court proceedings and the eventual eviction of the tenant, it is unlikely the landlord will be able to recover any of the lost rent.

You may also have to pay back some of the rent you have received

If the claimant has been receiving benefits that he is not entitled to and has been making false claims about his circumstances, the local authority can demand that you pay back the rent you have received from them. This condition can only be applied if the rent has been paid directly to you and not the tenant.

What happens if the tenant has already left the property?
Even if the tenant has left the property, you will still have to repay
the rent overpayment, or part of it, for the period when the tenant
was in residence. If you are housing another benefit tenant, the
local authority can deduct the repayment debt from that rent! It
may not be fair but the local authority can do it and they will.

What if the rent is paid directly to the managing agent?
The landlord is still obliged to pay back to the local authority the
overpayment. However, if the landlord cannot be traced, the
responsibility will fall to the managing agent. Many agents refuse
to accept payments made directly to them and will make provision
for the landlord to receive direct payments only. This way, they
absolve themselves of any repayment responsibilities.

TIP

Before taking on such a tenancy always check with your lease and insurance that
no restrictions are in place preventing this kind of occupancy.

RENTING OUT YOUR FORMER RESIDENCE

Should you find yourself in a position where you are re-located for
any length of time or for any reason you choose not to live in
your property, make sure you tell your mortgage lender. Strictly
speaking, a domestic property should not be rented out. Inform
the lender and, if it is to be short term, six months or so, the
lender may decide to let you keep the same mortgage. Some
lenders, however, may take the view that the property has become
a buy to let and adjust the interest accordingly.

If the rental period is liable to be longer, you will almost certainly
be required to change your mortgage, as your property will be

seen as a designated buy to let. If you choose to return to live in your property, you will have to change your mortgage back again when you take up occupancy. There will also be tax implications. If you are making money from your home, you cannot claim tax relief as you can with a buy to let mortgage.

TAXATION

If you become a private landlord, your tax position may be affected. Any profit you make on the rent of your property will be taxable. If you sell your property, you will be subject to capital gains tax. Taxation can vary according to your individual circumstances. Consult your accountant or financial advisor for more information. If you do not have an accountant, get in touch with your local tax office or visit www.inlandrevenue.gov.uk for advice. Tax issues will, however, be covered in greater detail in Chapter 6.

INVESTING IN BUY TO LET FOR CAPITAL GROWTH

This is when you invest in a property, where the anticipated yield of that property will not cover the mortgage or make you any income. In fact, the property could be termed as a liability, rather than an asset because it actually costs you money to rent it out. This situation is common in inner city areas, where rental markets are saturated.

What are the advantages of buying a property like this?

If you are buying a property that is costing you money to run, it will be because you believe that property will increase in value enough to cover losses and net you a handsome capital gain when you choose to sell it. There is no reason to suspect that this will not happen in a rising market. If the market falls, however, you could end up in a negative equity situation, with the cost of the property being more than it is worth when you want to sell it. Obviously, if the market is falling, it is better to hang onto the property if you can but this will be entirely dependent on your own personal circumstances.

LET TO BUY

This can be another way of building up your property portfolio. It is the reverse of buy to let – instead of selling your own house when you re-locate, you re-mortgage, refurbish and then rent it out. This way you own two homes, one which you are living in, the other which you are renting out, ideally for enough money to cover your mortgage and net you an income. It also means that when you come to sell either property, you will be entitled to Tapered Capital Gains Relief, depending on how long you have lived in each property.

SUMMARY

Buy to let, in my opinion, still represents a good investment opportunity, as long as you do your research and follow a few simple rules:

- Only purchase in areas where there is strong rental demand.

- Buy in areas next to 'hotspots'.

- Buy near amenities, schools, shops, restaurants, offices.

- Buy near good transport links.

- Speak to estate agents to find out what kind of properties are in demand in the area.

- Find out if they are busy. How many vacant apartments do they have on their books?

- Read the local papers and get property rental lists from all agents in the area.

- Get agents to send you details of properties that match your requirements.

- Work out the returns from home and if everything stacks up, then you can confidently go ahead with your purchase.

Buying Off Plan

If you are of a nervous disposition, then 'buying off plan' is probably not for you. If, however, you are serious about being a property millionaire and can live with the odd sleepless night, buying off plan is an option you should consider when choosing to invest in the property market.

WHAT DOES BUYING OFF PLAN ACTUALLY MEAN?

'Buying off plan' means a leap of faith because you are buying a property that hasn't yet been built. You are, literally, buying the property off a plan. This 'plan' will generally contain details of the layout, the square footage and the specification of the property.

It is the developer's job to tempt you into taking that leap of faith and part with your cash. In order for them to do this, there will generally be a marketing strategy which will involve glossy brochures, high profile advertising, models of the proposed development, computer generated images and an 'all singing, all dancing' show flat. The purpose of all this glitz is to make their product look as attractive as possible, in order to lure you into investing in their development.

Seeing through the glitz

It is your job to investigate all the areas, when buying off plan, that will maximise your 'property profit potential'. A glitzy package may not always represent the best investment. This chapter is designed to help you make informed decisions about the real selling points of a development and to help you purchase your property at below market value.

WHY BUY OFF PLAN?

The principle reason to buy off plan is to achieve a discount of around 20% off the market value of the property. This is generally possible, especially in a rising market, because the property is only in the construction or pre-construction stage at the time of purchase. This will mean that there is a 'lead in time' whilst the property is being built, which will last until construction is completed and the property is ready for occupation. This 'lead in time', can vary from a year or more, depending on the construction schedule.

How do I know if I am getting the off plan property at a discount?

Research the price of similar properties in the same location. If you consider that the developer is asking too much of a premium for the off plan property, let them know that you have done your homework, researched the area and that you consider their price to be inflated. Be prepared to put in an offer below the asking price – the worst they can do is refuse it and if they don't refuse it, then you've got a property at a reduced price.

TIP

If the developer refuses to budge on the price, or offer any incentives to buy, and you genuinely believe the property to be overpriced, then don't buy it. There are always other properties to consider and your aim is to make the correct business decision that will enable you to maximise 'property profit potential'.

Are there any other ways I can secure a discount when buying off plan?

The best time to maximise on any discount possibilities likely to be offered is at the beginning of the development. It is then that you get the first pick of the units at the best price. This has involved people queuing outside a development overnight, in order to get the best deals! It is worth considering this if you are optimistic that the development will be popular (and are young enough to be able to stand it!). I must admit that I have never queued overnight but I have been up extra early and it has enabled me to get some good deals.

Case study

I was recently offered the opportunity of investing in an apartment block in Manchester. The apartments were priced significantly lower than similar properties in the area and the developer was expecting an overwhelming response. The selling agent for the developer was so confident that people would be queuing overnight for the properties, he suggested I employ someone to do the queuing on my behalf, if I seriously wanted to buy.

TIP

Although employing someone to queue for you overnight to purchase a property may seem extreme, it is certainly a consideration, if you want to have the pick of the crop at the best price within the development of your choice. If you want a bargain, you will have to put yourself out to get one, as you will not be the only one wanting to buy properties below their market value.

Being invited to buy at a substantially discounted price

This is often reserved exclusively for what I like to refer to, as the 'high rollers', the big investors, where it is not uncommon for them to buy a hundred units at a time. Not only do they get a discount, they also put down a smaller deposit and get to choose their units before anyone else. In addition they get to choose units in different stages of the development and not all in the first phase, when the majority of the development could still be a building site, making it difficult to rent out and inconvenient to live in. Being a 'high roller' is what every would be property investor should aspire to, because joining that exclusive club is how you get the best deals.

GETTING IN PRE-LAUNCH

Another way of securing your discount is to 'get in' before the development is officially launched or released. In order to do this, it is important to familiarise yourself with estate agents in the area. Some of the larger agencies will have a direct link with the developer and may well be selling some units off at discounted prices, prior to release. These will be offered to 'preferred' buyers, people who are serious about investing.

TIP

Let the estate agent know that you are a serious buyer, unencumbered and able to secure a mortgage. Keep in contact with them and let them know that you are keen. They will put you on their 'hot list' and inform you when the first units are being sold.

Being on an estate agent's 'hot list'

This is a good place to be, particularly if you are serious about investing in the property market. However, if an estate agent is offering you an early 'in' to a development, at a discounted price, do not be afraid to negotiate further. You may not get anything off the asking price but you may be able to negotiate only putting down a 5% deposit. Most estate agents work on commission and they want your business, not only for this development but for future ones, so it's in their interests to keep you sweet.

Case study

I once purchased an apartment 'pre-launch' in Liverpool. I asked to put down a 5% deposit instead of the required 10%. My request to do this was turned down by the developer and the selling agent. However, I was confident that the development would prove to be popular and rather than agree to pay the 10%, I negotiated to purchase two units instead of one, on the condition that I would only have to pay a 5% deposit on each. In essence, I got two units for the price of one, and was successful in selling both units prior to completion, thus netting myself double the profit, for half the outlay.

Why would a developer pre-release off plan properties?
A pre-launch is a useful opportunity for the developer to test the water, pricewise. If the pre-launch goes well then you can bet your 'en suite bathroom' that they will up the prices for the launch!

BUYING AT THE LAUNCH
By now, the developer may well have sold some of the units through the ways listed above. This is not always the case and now it really is a matter of first come, first served. If some of the units have been pre-sold, it does not mean that there aren't good deals

to be had when the development is launched to the public. The pre-launch sales may not have got off to a good start if the properties have been priced too high, or not had the market appeal that the developer had hoped for. If, on the other hand, the pre-launch sales were a success, your negotiating powers at the launch will be reduced and you will have to negotiate hard to get the best deal you can.

Case study

I once bought an apartment 'off plan' identical to my subsequent neighbours. They did not negotiate and paid full price for their apartment. I paid the same amount but negotiated incentives (to have a parking space and wooden floors thrown in as part of the deal). By doing this, I netted myself a substantial discount on the market value of the property and maximised the 'property profit potential'.

Incentives

These are baubles dangled in front of you to tempt you to buy. They can range from upgraded appliances, free flooring throughout, furniture packs and sometimes a car parking space. Other incentives are cash back schemes, guaranteed rental packages, 5% deposits, stamp duty paid and part exchange deals, to name but a few. One thing a developer does not want to be seen to be doing is actually lowering their prices from the launch. Therefore, incentives are offered, which are really just disguised discounts. These 'discounts' can be increased by the developer at any time, if sales are going through a sluggish period.

The more incentives you are offered, the bigger your discount will be. Some incentives will be offered as part of the deal but it is always worth asking for extra incentives. If they won't throw in a car parking space, maybe you could ask for your stamp duty to be paid instead?

Buying at the end of the development

This can be a good time to go with your shopping basket to pick up a bargain, but it is important that you assess why the last remaining units haven't sold. If the property is still in the building process and you can't walk round it, ask how soon you can. Make sure you have carefully studied all the plans relating to the property, as there must be a reason why the last units have not sold. This could be because of asking price, aspect or location within the development.

Often it can be the more expensive units that 'stick'. The developer will generally offer significant discounts at the end of a development, in order to shift these units. Once all the units are sold, they can close the marketing suite and move on!

Buying in a completed development

If the development is complete, you will be able to visit the property in person and walk around it yourself, without having to try and imagine how it will look. You can then decide whether you are interested in buying. If you are interested, you should be in a position to drive a hard bargain.

WHAT OTHER FACTORS SHOULD I CONSIDER?

To buy off plan successfully, it is wise to make an informed decision, not a spur of the moment one, and this means studying the floor plans in detail. Square footage, specification, location, aspect and reputation of the developer are all important points to consider before going ahead with your purchase.

Square footage/floor plans

In inner cities, where space is at a premium, apartments are getting smaller and smaller. Some are described as smart pads, crash pads, pods, suites or studios. The square footage of these studio type apartments can vary from 250 sq. ft to 530 sq. ft, the latter being larger than some one-bedroom apartments, but most will hover around the 300 sq. ft mark.

TIP

If you are considering buying a small studio apartment off plan, make sure you physically pace out exactly what your living space will be, as this is hard to visualise from a floor plan. Think where your furniture will go and how much room you will have, once the room has a bed in it. Take time to consider exactly what living in such a small space will mean and whether or not compact living is for you. If you are planning to rent out the property, consider whether it would appeal to potential tenants.

One bedroom apartments

One bedroom apartments can range in size from 450 sq. ft to 600 sq. ft and again, it is advisable to pace out your living space. The bedrooms in smaller one bedroom apartments can be cramped and often only have room for a small double bed and single wardrobe. In show flats, they will often disguise the true size of rooms with custom made furniture and clever use of mirrors. Try to look beyond the glamorous image of the show flat and imagine how your furniture will fit. Is there going to be sufficient room for that family heirloom, for instance?

If you are planning to rent out the property, does it have any storage? Quite often in modern apartment blocks, storage is low down on the list of priorities – check if there is anywhere to put the vacuum cleaner.

Two bedroom apartments

Two bedroom apartments can vary considerably in size and can range from approximately 640 sq. ft to 1,000 sq. ft. A lot of two bedroom apartments will have an en-suite bathroom plus a guest bathroom, and this can result in the actual living space being cut down quite considerably. Two bathrooms, on the other hand, are very useful if you are considering renting the property out.

Three bedroom apartments

Three bedroom apartments can be from 1,000 sq. ft upwards and loft apartments can range from 1,000 sq. ft to in excess of 2,000 sq. ft. The general rule is that the larger the property is, within a mixed unit development, the cheaper per square foot it will be. This is because the larger units will be the more expensive ones to buy and therefore will appeal to a smaller market. This is a developer's way of offering a sweetener to tempt buyers to invest in the larger units.

Houses

A middle market house on a new development will generally be more generous in size than an apartment. The living space can range from anything between 1,000 sq. ft to 1,500 sq. ft. Consider carefully the size of each room and whether or not the bedrooms will accommodate a growing family. Houses tend to aim for this kind of market. A small bedroom may be suitable for a toddler but may not meet the demands of a teenager. It is advisable when purchasing a family house off plan to consider whether it will meet a growing family's needs or those of your future tenants.

TIP

When buying off plan, always take time to try and visualise the space you are buying. If you don't, you may come to regret your purchase when you move in and find the property to be much smaller in actuality than what you had hoped. Remember, developers are out to make as much money as possible, so they will try to squeeze as many units out of a development as they can get away with. If you are in any doubt about proposed room sizes, always pace it out. If you don't have an area big enough to pace out the size of the living space, try the local park – you may get a few strange looks from passers-by but it will be worth it in the end!

Specification

Specification defines the standard of finishes for white goods, flooring, worktops, bathrooms, etc. that can be expected once the apartment/house is complete. A fairly standard specification will read as follows:

Internal doors
Wood veneered ash

Ironmongery
In polished chrome

Kitchen
Cabinets in a gloss white with chrome trim and polished chrome handles

Appliances
Stainless steel microwave
Stainless steel oven
Electric hob
Stainless steel cooker hood
Washer/dryer
Stainless steel dishwasher
Upright fridge freezer

Ceramic wall tiling
Kitchen, main bathroom, en-suite, shower room and WC

Floor covering
Maple strip wood in kitchen, lounge and dining area

Carpets
Carpets in hallway, bedrooms and dressing rooms

Internal finishes
White matt vinyl in kitchen and bathrooms
Almond white matt vinyl for all remaining walls

Specifications vary widely from development to development. Some developers may offer only the most basic of finishes, whilst others will offer, not only top of the range appliances, but anything from plasma screen televisions to roof-top swimming pools. Obviously the better the 'spec' the more you will pay. Whether you choose to buy into a 'high spec' development will be a decision that will be based on whether you intend to buy the property as an investment or intend to live there yourself.

> ### TIP
> The higher the specification the more you will pay – there is no such thing as a free lunch. So rest assured that if granite worktops are included in the specifications, they will almost certainly have been covered by the overall price of the unit.

Case study
Other specifications will miss out certain items, so it is advisable to read what's on offer with a keen eye. I recently purchased a house in a mixed unit development which I thought came with a washer/dryer, only to discover that this appliance came with the apartments only. This was easy to miss, as the rest of the specification did not differentiate in any other way between the houses and the apartments. Even though I am experienced in reading specifications, I can still be caught out! Had I known the house was not going to be fitted with this appliance I would have negotiated for it as an incentive to buy.

Bespoke service

Some developers offer a bespoke service. This is a good way for the developer to raise extra revenue and an expensive way for the buyer to upgrade the developers' original specification. The developer can offer such things as upgraded work surfaces, designer bathroom tiles, washer/dryers and integrated cappuccino makers! If the apartment comes without flooring, they will offer a choice of wood floors and carpets. All these items will be deemed as extras and, as such, you will have to pay an extra price to have them.

It will, of course, be up to you whether you choose to opt for an upgraded specification but you will almost certainly find, particularly with the flooring, that you would be able to purchase these items cheaper elsewhere. So shop around!

The reputation of the developer

If you know the developer and have bought from them before, then all well and good. You are obviously satisfied with their work, otherwise you would not be buying another property from them! If, however, you are not familiar with their reputation, it is worth taking a look at their history. You can generally check this out on the Internet. If it is a large developer they will probably have other developments that you can have a look at, to give you an idea of the standard of the building work. This will also enable you to see how well or badly the development is wearing.

Try to talk to residents and see if they are happy living in the development, or if they are experiencing problems. If the developer is small or relatively new and doesn't have a track record, you will have to make a brave choice, but make sure they are covered by proper insurance.

Aspect

It is difficult to visualise what kind of views your off plan house or apartment will have but it is essential to do this, otherwise you could end up making a costly mistake. Think about the development as a whole and where your property is positioned within it. If it's on the ground floor, will it overlook the bin store or the car park (not always a bad thing if you have an expensive car!)? Where is the proposed development to be located – is it next to a council block, scrap yard, rubbish tip or restaurant? These are questions you should find out the answers to, particularly in inner city areas where space is at a premium and developments are crowded on top of each other.

TIP

If the sales office/show flat is not situated on site, visit the proposed development's location yourself and have a good look around.

Higher floors

If you are purchasing a property on one of the higher floors, you will pay a premium, approximately £3,000 to £5,000 + per floor the higher you go. It will be hard to visualise the view but try to imagine what it would be like to look out of your window. For instance, if there is a block of flats in front of the proposed development, will your apartment look over the top? It may be worth paying a premium to be on a higher floor that does. If you are buying an apartment in a development where some of the flats enjoy river views and others don't, this will obviously be reflected in the purchase price.

Where does the sun rise and set?

This is important if you want the property to enjoy the sun and have natural light. One of the major reasons basement flats are not desirable, apart from damp, is lack of light. So don't forget to consider the light/sun factor when purchasing your off plan investment. It may not seem important to you when you are being seduced by the show flat but it will be important once you start to live in the property or rent it out.

Maximising property profit potential

You should consider carefully when choosing your apartment/house which unit will maximise your 'property profit potential' most. Mid-priced properties fit this criteria the best, as they will appeal to a larger market and this in turn will increase your future selling/renting prospects.

Service charge

Most of the developers will have estimated a service charge in relation to the apartment you have chosen to buy. This will be based on square footage and what facilities the development is proposing to offer. If the development has a swimming pool and gym, 24-hour porterage and valet parking, your service charge will be higher than in a development that offers some or none of these facilities. You will also, within your service charge, pay for the management company to run the apartment block. If you expect the development to be maintained to a high standard, you will be required to cover this in your contribution to the annual service charge.

Purchasing the freehold

In most new schemes, for the first two years the responsibility for the management of the development will belong to the developer and it will be up to them to appoint a managing agent. After this initial period, the managing agent could change or in certain cases you could be offered a chance to purchase a share in the freehold. If you are offered a share of the freehold and have the requisite number of owner-occupiers interested in purchasing, I would always try to do this. It gives you more of a say in how the development is run, is more economical and is a good selling point, which all adds to the overall 'property profit potential'.

WHAT IS THE NORMAL PROCEDURE WHEN BUYING OFF PLAN?

◆ **Reservation fee**. The apartment of your choice is reserved for you and you will be expected to pay a non-returnable reservation fee of between £1,000 and £2,500.

◆ **Insurance**. Before you hand over the fee, check whether the developer is NHBC or registered with Zurich. This means that the developer is insured against lost deposits and will have to build the development to a certain standard before they are allowed to 'sign off' on the property. This will also mean that your property will have a two year 'snagging' guarantee and a ten year structural one.

◆ **Solicitors**. The developer may often have a preferred solicitor who may be able to offer you discounted legal fees. If, however, you have your own solicitors and you like them, then stick with them. It will mean that you are confident that someone you know and trust is looking after your interests.

◆ **Deposit**. A deposit of 5–10% is required on exchange of contracts.

◆ **The exchange of contracts** will generally take place within a 28-day period. If you fail to complete on the property, you will automatically lose the deposit!

◆ **Completion date**. An estimated completion date for the property will be agreed but this will be when the property is finished, and almost all developers fall behind schedule. The completion date is a target time, which the developer wants to hit as much as you. If the building programme falls behind schedule, there is not much you can do about it except wait ... patiently!

- **The hand-over**. You will be notified 10 to 14 days before completion is to take place. This may not be convenient for you. You may have booked a holiday, or the development might still be a building site, but if the developer wants to complete and the property has been signed off by the NHBC (assuming it is covered by them) then you will have to complete, whether you like it or not.

- The Council of Mortgage Lenders brought in new **guidelines** in 2002 and developments now have to comply with much stricter regulations. Whatever floor the apartment is on, the building has to have fully functioning common parts and the lifts must be working upon completion. This does not mean to say that leisure facilities, restaurants (always proposed) will be up and running. Far from it – they could still be a long way off, particularly if you bought in the first phase.

- **Stamp duty** will be payable on completion.

- **Snagging**. During the 10 to 14 days notice period you will be invited into the property to do a 'snagging' list. Although a property is brand new, it can quite often have many faults and it is up to the developer to put these faults right within a guaranteed two-year period from the completion date.

- **After sales**. You need to be very thorough when doing the 'snagging' and if there is anything you are not happy with, make sure it is listed. If you have a long 'snagging' list, as you generally will have (certainly in my experience), then these things will not all necessarily be put right before your moving in day. There is not much you can do about this, as you will still have to complete, but any such outstanding issues should only be minor. If they are of a more serious nature, you should seek the advice of your solicitor.

IS THERE A DOWNSIDE TO BUYING OFF PLAN?

The value of property goes down as well as up, and if you purchase a property off plan, you could end up paying more for it than it will be worth by the time it is complete. This could result in you having difficulty raising a full mortgage on the property. If you have to default on the contract, you will lose your deposit. Keep an eye on what is happening to the property market during the build programme; market forces could have changed and you could end up with negative equity. If this is a possibility, think very carefully how you will finance the mortgage shortfall and whether or not you will have to sell on and take a loss. It is always worth speaking to the developer if you find yourself in this difficult situation, as they may be able to help.

FINALLY

I have to confess to being like a kid in a sweet shop when it comes to buying off plan. I get excited by show flats, glossy brochures, state of the art kitchens, bathrooms, granite work surfaces, limestone, walnut, stainless steel and glass ... lots of glass. It's amazing to see what the developers will come up with next in order to steal a march on the competition. However, buying off plan is a serious investment and tempting though the glitz may be, don't get carried away by it. If you are not sure that a property is a good investment, walk away from it. Being prepared to walk away from a deal is not only the strongest negotiating tool of all, it is also sound business sense. If you want to build a property portfolio worth in excess of a million pounds, you must not be tempted to pay over the odds for any property, no matter how much you like it!

You won't become a property millionaire overnight, but buying an off plan property at a discounted price will enable you to sell on your property at a profit, in a rising market. An alternative to selling the property is to rent it out and re-mortgage. Raise capital to buy another property, which will enable you to begin to build a property portfolio.

SUMMARY

Buying off plan can be a good option for the budding property millionaire, but make sure you check the plan and specifications thoroughly. Take time to visualise what the apartment or house will be like once it is finished, and don't be afraid to negotiate.

6

Your Tax Liability

As a property investor, you will be required to pay tax on your profits. Tax regulations are constantly changing so another important member of your team will be an accountant. Accountants vary in specialisation and temperament and you need to shop around to find one who has specialist knowledge of the property market and who will instinctively give you, as an entrepreneur, good advice. Accountancy is a retrospective practice and not many of them have an entrepreneurial spirit, but there are good ones out there who will embrace what you are trying to do and help you manage both your business and tax planning efficiently.

There are huge savings to be made if you deal with tax in the correct way but I would not advise tax avoidance schemes, as these are expensive to set up and have a habit of catching you out. This chapter can only deal with tax in general terms and you would be advised to consult your accountant regarding your individual tax circumstances.

WHAT TAXES WILL I HAVE TO PAY?

There are a variety of taxes that apply to property. The main ones of concern are stamp duty, capital gains, VAT and income tax. When you buy a property you have to pay stamp duty. The rate of this can be changed by the Chancellor in his Budget and has been increased in recent years. If you sell a property that is not your 'primary residence', you will have to pay capital gains tax. If you make a profit on the rentals you will be liable for income tax.

STAMP DUTY

Current rates of tax payable on property fall within these bands:

Purchase not exceeding £60,000	Nil
Purchase between £60,000 and £250,000	1%
Purchase between £250,001 and £500,000	3%
Purchase over £500,001	4%

Obviously, it is in your interest when buying a property that you do not pay a small amount over any of these thresholds, as it will cost you more in tax. This explains why there is an enormous sticking point at £250,000.

Example

If you buy a property for £250,500 it will cost you £258,015, including £7,515 in tax. If you negotiate the price down to £250,000 then you will pay £2,500 in tax.

Trying to keep below a threshold

The Inland Revenue is now very aware of this and it is difficult to do deals by paying cash for fixtures and fittings. There may be some leeway in specific cases, but you should always consult your lawyer and accountant rather than risk falling foul of the Revenue.

INCOME TAX

Income tax is payable on any profits that you make from your property dealing. The Inland Revenue now operates a self assessment system and it is your responsibility to report your income and expenses to the Revenue for each year ending the 5th April. Rents are defined as income and against this you can charge a variety of allowable expenses.

Claimable expenses

The general guide is that all allowable expenses have to be 'wholly and exclusively' for the purposes of the property and it gets confusing if they are shared. Examples of legitimate expenses are:

- interest payments on mortgage
- letting agent fees
- legal and professional fees
- ground rent and service charges
- insurance
- cleaning
- wear and tear allowance of 10% of gross rent received – if the property is furnished.

Income versus capital

You need to be aware which expenses can be put against income and which apply to the capital value of the property. Renovations apply to the capital value, as do legal costs incurred in the purchase or sale of properties. These expenses cannot be claimed for, as they are judged to be part of the capital costs and are added to the price of the property for capital gains purposes. Similarly you cannot claim for purchasing furnishings, as this is covered by the 10% wear and tear allowance.

TIP

Losses can be carried forward from one year to another. So, if at the start of your rentals you are making a loss, this amount can be offset in the years in which you make a profit.

CAPITAL GAINS TAX

You do not have to pay capital gains tax on the sale of your main residence. You will have to pay capital gains tax on any other property that you sell for a profit, in excess of your personal allowances. At the last Budget the personal allowance was raised to £8,200 per person per year. This amount cannot be carried forward to another year but it does apply to joint owners of a property. This means that if you and your partner jointly own a property you will not have to pay tax on the first £16,400.

Advantages

The advantage of investing in property is that there are certain allowances available against capital gains tax. Because of the complexities of the tax structure this is quite complicated. There are a lot of special stipulations and allowances that are worth understanding, as you can save a great deal of money if you think things through in advance. Firstly, you have to work out what the property cost.

Cost of the property
- The purchase price of the property.
- Acquisition costs – legal fees, stamp duty, searches, etc.
- Renovation or enhancement – this is structural and not surface. A new roof, double glazed windows or an extension are all acceptable allowances but new carpets and curtains are not.
- Add all these items together and you have the cost of the property.

Special stipulations
This depends on when you bought the property, as there a number of allowances that you can add to the cost of the property before calculating the 'true cost' for tax purposes.

Property bought before 31st March 1982

Capital gains tax was restructured at this time, so any increase in value before this period is non-taxable.

- If you bought a property for rental in 1972 for £15,000 and spent £5,000 on enhancement expenditure, the value of the property would have been £20,000.

- If you sold it in 2002 for £200,000 the capital gain would be based on its actual value at 31st March 1982, which for the purposes of this example we'll say is £30,000.

- Therefore the gain is £170,000 not £180,000. (The taxman likes to have his cake and eat it too.)

- If the value of the property fell between the actual purchase price of £20,000 to £15,000 on 31st March 1982, the taxable gain would be taken as the highest figure – in this case the £20,000.

Indexation reliefs

For the period from March 1982 to April 1998 the situation was changed to a tax relief known as indexation, which was linked to the inflation rate on the Retail Prices Index. A chart is printed at end of this chapter to show the rate on an annual basis. It adds up to 104.7% over the whole period.

Example
- A property was valued at £30,000 in March 1982, leaving a gain of £170,000.
- It was sold after April 1998, therefore the full indexation relief is allowable.
- So £30,000 × 104.7% equals £31,410.
- Subtract this from £170,000.
- The gain is reduced to £138,590.

Taper relief

Now just to make things more complicated the rules changed from April 1998 and taper relief was introduced. Residential property investments are classed as 'non-business assets', so qualify on a fixed annual rate as follows:

Property held less than 3 years	Nil
Property held for 3 years but less than 4	5%
Property held for 4 years but less than 5	10%
Property held for 5 years but less than 6	15%
Property held for 6 years but less than 7	20%
Property held for 7 years but less than 8	25%
Property held for 8 years but less than 9	30%
Property held for 9 years but less than 10	35%
Property held for 10 years or more	40%

If you held the property from before 17th March 1998, you are allowed to add an extra year onto the above formula.

Example
- The period before April 1998 is disregarded, so since the property was owned before March 1998, an extra year is added on.
- March 1998 to the sale date of April 2003 is 5 years, plus the 'extra' year which makes 6 years and therefore 20% relief.
- The pre-tapered gain of £138,950 is multiplied by 20%.
- This equals £27,718.
- Resulting in a gain of £110,872.

At what rate is capital gains tax charged?

The annual exemption is changed in the Budget each year, in line with inflation, and currently stands at £8,200 for each individual.

The rate, thereafter, is dependent on your income. A higher rate tax payer will pay 40%. If you have no taxable income the rates will be calculated as follows:

The first £2,020	10%
The next £29,380	20%
Thereafter	40%

Example
- On your gain of £110,872, subtract your allowance of £8,200.
- This leaves a net gain of £102,672.
- If you are a higher rate tax payer at 40% you will have to pay £41,068 capital gains tax to the Inland Revenue by 31st January of the year in which it was due.

How can I pay less capital gains tax?
The easiest way is to co-own your property with your partner. Their personal allowance can be added to yours and if they have no income, the sums look even more promising. If you have transferred the property into joint names early enough, so that the partner has had a genuine beneficial title, then it is deemed to be owned equally. However, you cannot transfer the property into joint names just before the sale takes place.

Example
- The gain on the sale of the property was £110,872.
- Divide this in two halves of £55,436.
- Firstly the 'non-incomed' partner:
- £55,436 minus £8,200 = £47,236.
- The first £2,020 at 10%   £202
- The next £29,380 at 20%   £5,876
- The remainder (£47,236 – £31,400) £15,836 at 40%   £6,334
- Total tax for the 'non-incomed' partner   £12,412

* Secondly the 40% tax payer
* £55,436 minus £8,200 = £47,236 × 40%   <u>£18,894</u>
* **Total tax bill**   **£31,306**
* You have paid £31,306 instead of £41,068, which equals a saving of £9,762, by having the property in joint ownership.

When the property is your primary private residence

As ever, there are a number of ways to reduce your tax bill. For example, by having lived in the property, as your primary private residence (PPR), before or after renting it out and provided the property is genuinely your primary residence, no capital gains tax is paid. The following criteria have to be met for the property to become your PPR.

* You, your partner and your family have to live in the property for a substantial period.
* You must be registered on the Electoral Roll at this address.
* You must be registered at this address with all relevant institutions such as bank, utilities and the Inland Revenue.
* Family and friends treat it as your primary address.
* You furnish it for permanent occupation.

TIP

If you want maximum property profit potential, don't put the property up for sale or rent until you have lived there for at least a year.

Renovating and moving on

A very successful way to get a sizeable capital sum is to buy a run-down property and renovate it, whilst living in it. Then you can sell it or rent it out and move into another property that needs renovation. Your capital is increasing and no capital gains tax (CGT) is paid at all.

What if I used to live in the property and then rented it out?

Again there are benefits to having lived in the property at some time in the past. The PPR exemption covers the period when it was your main residence, plus the last three years of ownership. So, if you rented out the property for three years after moving out, there is no CGT to pay at all. If you rent it for longer than three years, another relief kicks in: private letting relief.

Private letting relief

This is described as being the lowest of:

- ◆ The amount of gain already exempted under PPR.
- ◆ The gain arising over the letting period.
- ◆ £40,000.

Example
- ◆ You bought a property in 1994 for £100,000, lived in it for five years and rented it out for five years.
- ◆ In 2004 you sold it for £180,000.
- ◆ The gain is £80,000, of which 5/10ths is covered by PPR and the other 5/10ths – £40,000 – is private letting relief.
- ◆ As a result there is no CGT to pay at all.

What happens if I rented out the property and then lived in it?

A property that qualifies for partial exemption under PPR is treated exactly the same, whenever it was your main residence.

What about second homes?

When you buy a second home you are allowed two years, from when it becomes available to you as a main residence, to register either one of your properties with your Tax Office as your PPR.

Example
You have a flat in London and buy a holiday cottage in
Whitstable. Due to the popularity of the area the holiday home is
increasing in value at a greater rate than the London property. In
the second year you elect to make the Whitstable property your
main PPR. When you sell it there is no CGT to pay. You then re-
register your London property as your primary residence.

Holiday lets

If you let out a furnished holiday home it is counted as a trade.
This means that there are further tax advantages, as it qualifies
for 'Business Asset Taper Relief'. In order to qualify the following
criteria must be met:

- The property must be furnished.
- It must be available for commercial letting for at least 140 days
  in a 12-month period.
- It must be let out for at least 70 days in a 12-month period.
- It must not be let out to the same occupants for more than 31
  days consecutively at any time during a period of seven months
  out of the same 12-month period as above.
- The property must be in the UK.
- The 12-month period is usually the tax year.

Income tax
Again, income tax is payable on profits. However, unlike buy to
let, losses can be charged against the owner's profits on their other
business.

Capital gains tax
As the holiday let qualifies as a 'Business Asset' for CGT, like
commercial property, it qualifies for Business Asset Taper Relief,
which is more advantageous than relief for residential property.

Property held for less than one year   Nil
Property held for one year but less than 2 years   50%
Property held for two years or more   75%

VAT
Vat is not chargeable on rents. For income tax purposes the gross amount of expenses, including the VAT element, should be claimed.

TIP

If you are buying 'new build', you can claim back the VAT if you put in a wooden floor or fireplace (but not carpets) and only if you have the work done between the exchange and completion. Developers will usually let you do this work as you have committed to the purchase, even though you are not the outright owner. You will also want the work done before completion, so that you can rent it out quickly. So for once, it's a 'win win' scenario!

SHOULD I FORM A COMPANY?

The best advice I can give you for this is – it depends. This is a question for your accountant and you will need to get to grips with this question early on. If you want to transfer ownership of properties into a company at a later stage there are very expensive stamp duty payments that have to be paid. It all depends on the nature of your business and how you want to run it.

TIP

If you are buying and selling properties without doing any work to them – for example, selling on off plan properties – this is deemed to be a trade and should be done through a limited company, as the Inland Revenue might not let you claim your CGT allowance.

THE FUTURE

There are plans afoot in the April 2005 Budget to allow residential property to be held in a personal pension exempt from tax. This will be possible by setting up a SIPP – a Self-Invested Personal Pension – for retirement benefits, possibly free of capital gains tax, income tax and inheritance tax. This could apply to your existing buy to lets as well as new investments, which can be held in a pension fund. This could be very beneficial to the property investor.

CAPITAL GAINS TAX INDEXATION RELIEF RATES

Percentages applying to sales made after April 1998 of properties acquired during:

1982	97.1% to 104.7%
1983	87.1% to 96.8%
1984	78.9% to 87.1%
1985	69.3% to 78.3%
1986	63.2% to 68.9%
1987	57.4% to 62.6%
1988	47.4% to 57.4%
1989	36.9% to 46.5%
1990	25.2% to 36.1%
1991	19.8% to 24.9%
1992	16.8% to 19.9%
1993	14.6% to 17.9%
1994	11.4% to 15.1%
1995	7.9% to 11.4%
1996	5.3% to 8.3%
1997	1.6% to 5.3%
1998	0.0% to 1.9%

7

Investing in the North

I am from the North, so forgive me if I am biased, but I cannot help but be excited that northern cities are finally being regenerated on a grand scale. Far from being grim, the North can boast of museums, art galleries, improved transport links, high spec apartments, waterside living, shopping centres, expanding airports, bridges, new job opportunities and business initiatives. Northern cities are changing, are changing fast and are changing for the better. Hence the investor, with chequebook in hand, has started showing an interest and the floodgates for residential and commercial investment opportunities have opened.

WHY INVEST IN THE NORTH?

Property prices are cheaper, rental yields are higher. Northern cities are being regenerated. Property prices are rising in the North, while remaining static in most of the South. The economy in the North continues to boom and unemployment figures are low. There is also a genuine commitment from developers and local governments to increase cultural interests, facilities and transport links, in order to lure investors and increase job opportunities.

Relocation

Young single professionals from London are relocating to the North, working as accountants, lawyers, brokers and so on with companies that have satellite offices in Newcastle, Leeds, Manchester or Liverpool. Couples with children also relocate to the North because the region offers them the possibility of cashing in their London housing chips and buying a bigger house with a larger garden than they can afford in the South. There are also good schools in the North and these help attract families to relocate. Some businesses are also relocating northwards because business costs, staffing and overheads are lower than in South.

LOCAL MARKET FORCES

It is important, just as with the South, to understand as much as possible about local market forces. Take into consideration before choosing to invest what job opportunities are in the area. Does the area have a university? What are the plans for the infrastructure of the nearest town or city? Are regeneration schemes definitely planned? What is the master plan for the city?

The Northern Way

This is a proposed plan to link all the major northern cities as an 'extended metropolis', which could rival London in its economic power. Each city would retain its own identity, whilst together being seen as a single economic unit. This would attract business from the South, generate thousands of new jobs and relieve the housing pressure in the South.

In order for this long-term plan to work, it would necessitate new transport links, homes and business facilities. The new 'extended metropolis' would include the cities of Manchester, Leeds and Hull with spurs linking it to Sheffield in the south and Newcastle in the north. This plan is very much in its early stages but is an indication that the North is seen as an area of considerable investment potential.

Owner-occupiers/tenants
You will need to assess whether the property you choose to buy will have a market for either owner-occupiers to purchase or tenants for rental. The best investment property will appeal to both markets and this would be important in a downturn. If you wanted to sell the property and were unable to achieve the right price, you could put the property up for rental. Because of these factors a property that can satisfy both markets will always be the safer bet. This 'appealing to both markets' applies as much in the North as it does in the South.

HOW CAN I ASSESS WHICH NORTHERN CITY WOULD MAKE THE BEST INVESTMENT?
I always recommend visiting the city personally to get a 'feel' for the place. You can see with your own eyes whether the city centre is being regenerated or not by walking through it! Look out for skips, cranes and obvious signs of a building programme.

How big is the city?
This will obviously affect your market. The bigger the city, the bigger your market. This does not mean to say that there aren't good investments to be made in small towns and cities but obviously the market will not be as great. As more and more people choose to cut down on their commuting distance to work, living in the heart of a city affords that freedom. If a city has a large workforce and prospects of good future jobs growth, an investment property will have potential to increase in value in a rising market and a potential for rental should there be a downturn.

Theatre, cinema, museums and art galleries
If you want a good all round investment, it will be an advantage if

the city is on the 'up' and appeals to a wide market. If the city has a cultural aspect to it, how well is it represented? Does the city have museums and galleries to visit? Does it have a theatre, preferably one with an impressive track record? If the area does not have a cultural aspect to it, consider this when choosing your investment city, as this will affect your market. A thriving city should be able to accommodate most tastes.

Sport

Sport is an important part of our lives, whether we are football fans or not. Does the city have a well-supported football team? Are there any sports stadiums? Does the city host any major sporting events? Has the city got a dry ski slope nearby? These are questions that you can easily find the answers to and, although not necessarily conventional 'investor' questions, they can help you assess the morale of a city. If the leisure and sports facilities are good, the local population will be more stable than in a city where the services are poor.

Events

If a city hosts big events, this will not only make money for the city and create job opportunities but it will also keep it in the public eye. This, in turn, will help it to remain fashionable because a city will have to offer good facilities and infrastructure if it is to attract competitive business and music events.

Company investment

Are any 'household name' companies already in the area and are any planning to bring investment to the area, in the terms of new businesses and job creations? Your estate agent should be able to 'talk up' the area for you but if you want to verify any information for plans afoot, speak to the local authority planning department.

Industry and technology
Is the city famous for anything it produces, such as Sheffield, which is known for producing steel? Does it have active industries that manufacture goods? Does it have an expanding technology profile, which will create job opportunities and help bring long-term prosperity to the area? It is important to fully research what the employment situation is in any city and source where the areas for expansion are going to be. For instance, if you are aiming for a young professional to either rent or purchase your property, you will need to consider how central your property is to the business district of the city. If you are going to be renting to a student, you will need to consider the proximity of your property to a learning centre or university.

Change in working practices
A lot of cities are seeing a shift in their employment patterns. There are less manufacturing jobs and more in the service sector. The 'jobs for life' pattern has changed and the work force is more fluid, working on fixed term contracts or in a 'temporary' capacity. This does not mean that at the core, there isn't a stable workforce, but it means that in the service industries, such as in hairdressing, retail and catering, the work force is more transient and, as such, is more likely to rent in the short term.

History/attractions
What is the history of the city? Is it famous for any historical buildings? Does it have an interesting cathedral? Not all cities abound with ancient monuments but most should hold some

attraction for the visitor, even if it is only an excellent shopping centre!

Restaurants/cafes
Any city that has a plethora of coffee bars that spill out onto the pavement is moving with the times. The coffee industry is a big one and if a well-known coffee shop chain is going to open up in your area, this is a good sign. Most large chain concerns do their own extensive market research before they invest in an area. If they think that there is business to be had, then it shows a certain confidence in the area. Restaurants also play a large part in city living, as it is convenient for people to be able to walk to a good restaurant and not have to worry about the drink-driving issue. It is also important for visitors to the area to be able to enjoy a good standard of food during their visit and to be able to select from a wide variety of cuisines.

Famous people
Are any famous people from the city, such as the Beatles with Liverpool? Do any famous people live there? Do they promote the area? There is an obsession with fame and if a famous person chooses to come and nestle in the heart of a city, this can add to the appeal of city living. Living in the same block as a famous footballer can only add to the appeal, whether you like it or not!

What is the catchment area for the majority of the workforce?
This put quite simply is where people choose to live. If you buy a good property in an unfashionable area, this is unlikely to net you the same returns as if you choose a reasonable house in a fashionable area. How you determine what is fashionable and what isn't will of course be down to the proximity to facilities,

transport links and job opportunities in the area. Does the area have a visual edge? Is it close to a park, river or canal? If the property lies in a well-maintained part of the city, close to amenities and there are plans for improvements, this should represent a good investment in a rising market.

TIP

Most commuters choose not to travel too far to their place of work. Estimate journey times in relation to how far the property is from the city centre. The city centre will be a good indicator as to how central the property is, in relation to the majority of the workforce.

Road links
How far away is the city from a major road or motorway? What are the journey times from your chosen city to other major cities? How easy is it to get to London? Is the city easily accessible to Scotland, Ireland or Wales, as well as the capital?

Railways and airports
Are there efficient railway services to London and other major cities? Is there an airport close by? What cities are flown to and what are the journey times, destinations, costs? What are its European connections? Is the property you are considering conveniently placed for most transport links?

Crime rate
Does the city have a high crime rate and if so what areas are particularly affected?

New developments
How many new developments are planned? How many units are

being sold to 'investors'? If the majority of the development is being sold to investors then this could result in a glut of properties being released for rental, or for sale all at the same time. This would affect the market and you will need to consider whether you want to invest in such a block and whether you have the funds to ride out any new development hiccups, such as over-supply, low rental yields and failure to 'sell on' at the right price.

USEFUL INFORMATION ABOUT THE TOP NORTHERN CITIES

Below I have summarised some useful information about northern cities. There are many other factors to take into consideration when choosing to invest in the North but it would be impossible to list them all here. There are many websites which will aid your research and I have listed some of them here.

- UK cities local authorities: www.ukonline.gov.uk

- 2001 Census is a count of all people and households in the UK. It provides statistical information for schools, health services, roads and libraries: www.statistics.gov.uk/census2001

- Acorn Profiles (consumer preferences and behaviour). House price data can be accessed on www.upmystreet.com

- Regeneration profiles: www.englishpartnerships.co.uk

- Neighbourhood renewal office of the Deputy Prime Minister: www.neighbourhood.odpm.gov.uk

- Regeneration UK: www.regeneration-uk.com

Manchester

- The UK's second city, measured by population and business status.

- City centre population: 20,000.

- The city centre was bombed by the IRA in 1996 and has since been regenerated.

- Manchester hosted the Commonwealth Games in 2002 and this encouraged inner city investment.

- £83 million from public funding has been invested in the city centre.

- Piccadilly Station has undergone a £55m refurbishment.

- Public money has gone into museums and art galleries. Salford Quays has benefited from the modern Imperial War Museum North and the Lowry Arts Centre.

- Manchester Art Gallery was extended and a steel-strung bridge was erected over the Manchester Ship Canal.

- The sports facilities built for the Commonwealth Games have been put to good commercial use. The weight lifting venue is now the Manchester International Conference Centre, the four pool aquatic centre is now a public facility and the Commonwealth Stadium is now host to Manchester City FC.

- New retailers have moved in including Selfridges, Harvey Nichols and Heals.

- Blue chip companies are moving in and the rental market is maturing.

- The Beetham Tower is being built, which will be the highest residential building in the UK.

- Manchester is home to the famous Manchester United FC and Manchester City FC.

- It is also home to the excellent theatre, the Royal Exchange.

- Manchester has three universities (counting Salford).

- Manchester is famous for many things but particularly *Coronation Street*, which is recorded there (and I should know!).

- Manchester has trams and a good transport infrastructure.

TIP

There are nearly 9,000 city centre apartments, either occupied or nearing completion. The city centre has become expensive and over-subscribed with 'buy to let' investors. There are areas close to the city centre that have yet to reach their full potential in investment terms. As the city centre continues to thrive, the areas near to the boundaries of the centre can only benefit as the market widens to encompass these outer areas. Consider these areas when choosing your investment property.

Leeds
- Leeds is the UK's third largest city.

- Leeds is the largest financial centre outside London.

- Leeds has one of the fastest growing economies in the UK.

- A third of the city's £9 billion GDP is generated by the financial and business service sectors.

- It has offices for Price Waterhouse Cooper and KPMG business consultants.

- Most leading household names in retail banking and insurance services have offices there.

- Other financial companies there are First Direct, Alliance & Leicester, Halifax Direct and Direct Line as well as the long established GE Consumer Finance, which is the consumer lending and credit card division and has outlets in 35 different countries.

- It is the country's second major centre for paper manufacture, printing and publishing.

- It is the regional headquarters for supermarket giants ASDA and Morrisons.

- It has good state schools.

- It has regeneration prospects, with hundreds of city centre apartments currently under construction. Plans to revamp the Grand Theatre and Millenium Square, plus a new £26m museum.

- It has good transport links and is close to the MI, M6, M62, M621 and the A1.

- It has good train links to London and Scotland.

- It has two universities, a football team and the West Yorkshire Playhouse.

- It has urban waterfront areas.

- Leeds City Council forecasts a city centre population of over 16,000 in the next five years.

- Work has already started on the Supertram.

- The pedestrian heartland of Leeds attracts retail and leisure businesses.

- It boasts a Harvey Nichols and has designer, quirky shops and stalls at the Corn Exchange and Granary Wharf.

- Surrounding areas of Bradford, Harrogate, York, Huddersfield and Skipton are all within commuting distance of Leeds.

Newcastle/Gateshead
- The Gateshead Millennium Bridge cost £22m and leads directly to the entrance of the Baltic, a £46m centre for contemporary art.

- In 2005 the Sage Gateshead will open, a £70m music centre with two new concert halls and a music school.

- A new £7m dance centre will be opening in Newcastle with studios, theatre, library and café bar.

- The re-opening of The Waygood Gallery after a £5m refurbishment.

- The re-opening of the Newcastle Playhouse after a £7m rebuild.

- Tourism in the North East is now worth £1.6bn. It employs 100,000 people.

- It was one of the six short-listed cities for European Capital of Culture 2008.

- There is a council-funded 20 years regeneration initiative.

- It has a football club, good rugby clubs and is home to Jonny Wilkinson!

- It has Newcastle University and the University of Northumbria.

- The city centre is attracting trendy bars and restaurants.

- Newcastle has a history and was once a religious centre.

- The Council's Economy Development Strategy for the next ten years is to create a dynamic city offering opportunities for innovation, employment, business, education and leisure.

- The Quayside has been transformed and is now a vibrant cosmopolitan area.

- The transport system is the Tyne & Wear Metro.

- Newcastle has an airport.

Sheffield
- England's fourth largest city.

- Population of 550,000.

- Voted the safest city in the UK, according to government statistics.

- Sheffield's two universities teach 45,000 students annually.

- Sheffield College is the largest in Europe.

- One third of Sheffield is within the Peak District National Park.

- Sheffield is England's greenest city, containing 150 woodlands and 50 public parks.

- Sheffield Crucible Theatre has hosted the World Professional Snooker Championships every year since 1977. The Crucible Theatre itself is well respected for its dramatic productions and won the prestigious title of Barclays Theatre of the Year 2001.

- Sheffield Football Club is the oldest football club in the world.

- Over 500,000 tonnes of stainless steel is manufactured in Sheffield every year.

- Liquorice Allsorts – produced by Sheffield's sweet makers Cadbury Trebor Basset – celebrated 100 years of production in 1999.

- A large proportion of the world's surgical blades are made in Sheffield.

- A workforce of over 1 million people live within an hour's drive of the city.

- The Masterplan for Sheffield focuses on the city centre and includes, residential, retail, leisure and cultural facilities and improved transport links. The primary objective of the Masterplan is to create new jobs and to make sure that local communities have access to them. The fundamental principles of the Masterplan are:
  - To create excellent public places and facilities.
  - High quality commercial development including, hotel and offices to draw in private sector investment and create up to 1,500 new jobs.
  - City Hall is to be refurbished into a state-of-the-art, regionally important cultural venue and conference centre.
  - The new retail quarter will be pivotal to the Masterplan, the idea being, to lure high quality retailers and new shoppers back into the city centre and away from the shopping mall!
  - The railway station has an ongoing refurbishment plan.

TIP

Sheffield has a large student population, as well as its commercial sector. Students will not be able to afford high-spec city apartment living. A good investment could be to look for suitable student accommodation. This means properties priced at the lower end of the market and large enough to house sharers.

York

- York lies within one of the fastest growing economic areas in the UK.

- York is situated is just 21 miles from the financial capital of the North, which is Leeds.

- The city has established itself as a centre for high tech business, following the launch of the Science City York initiative in 1998. Since then it has created 1,600 new jobs with a further 15,000 new science and technology jobs expected to be created by 2021.

- York is 100 minutes from Kings Cross and 30 minutes from the Leeds/Bradford airport.

- The city has a strong financial and service sector.

- York has two universities and a law college.

- York has two theatres.

- York has a large tourist industry, as befits its Roman and medieval heritage.

- York Minster is a well-known attraction.

- The city has a racecourse.

- It has boutique shopping, good restaurants and trendy coffee bars.

- There are luxury apartments and town houses.

- York is situated within its historic wall.

- The average house price in York increased by 22.9% last year.

- York is an attractive city.

Liverpool

- Liverpool has been voted European Capital of Culture 2008.

- This will bring in £2bn of investment.

- £1.7m extra visitors.

- 14,000 new jobs.

- Liverpool has Europe's fastest growing airport, named after John Lennon.

- A new airline shuttle service 'The Liverbird', running daily trips to London, has been introduced and is already being hailed as a great success.

- Liverpool celebrates its 800th birthday in 2007.

- There is the connection with the Beatles.

- Liverpool is building a Fourth Grace, to compliment the Royal Liver Building, the Cunard Building and the Port of Liverpool Building.

- The city has theatres, museums and art galleries including the Tate.

- Liverpool has a two football clubs, Liverpool and Everton.

- Merseyside is among the UK's safest metropolitan areas, according to statistics from the Home Office.

- Liverpool has a university.

- Kings Waterfront is to be regenerated and will include a new conference centre, with adjacent arena and exhibition facility, hotels, residential and commercial development.

◆ The city has the famous Aintree racecourse, where the Grand National is hosted.

◆ Liverpool shipping group Bibby has secured £26m of funding to boost its UK operations and international expansion programme.

◆ Liverpool has two cathedrals.

FACTORS AFFECTING THE PROPERTY MARKET

The danger is, of course, that city apartments can be owned in large numbers by 'buy to let' investors, hoping to either 'flip' their property prior to completion or keep it to rent out, with the aim of achieving long-term capital gains. These factors can affect the stability of the market. First-time buyers will be priced out of the market, which will have a knock-on effect throughout the property chain.

If the market becomes saturated and there is an over-supply of properties for sale and rental, yield and sales prices will be automatically lowered. When this happens, the market has to shift outwards to the surrounding areas, within easy commuting distance of the city centre. It can be there that the best property bargains are to be had, if you are aiming to purchase at the lower end of the market.

If you are wanting to buy in a hotspot but are priced out, look at the area next to it. This will still be affordable and will have some capital gains potential, as the hotspot inevitably expands into the surrounding areas. Remember that in order to maximise on 'property profit potential', you are investing for long-term prospects, rather than short-term capital gains.

SUMMARY

Property prices are rising faster in the North than in the South, but are still relatively low. Many northern cities are being regenerated and workers and families are relocating there. Visit any areas you are considering investing in, think about all the factors listed in this chapter, then the decision is yours.

$$\left(\,8\,\right)$$

Estate Agents –
the Good, the Bad and the Ugly!

Estate agents are a necessary part of the property market and there are a lot of them out there. It is important that you choose the right one when selling or letting out your property. Anyone can set themselves up as an estate agent, so even if an agency appears to have all the trappings – flashy offices, headed notepaper, website – they may not have the track record to go with it.

GOOD ESTATE AGENTS

There is a choice of several organisations which a reputable estate agent should belong to and they are:

◆ NAEA, the National Association of Estate Agents
◆ ARLA, the Association of Residential Letting Agents
◆ NALS, the National Approved Letting Scheme
◆ RICS, the Royal Institute Of Chartered Surveyors.

Membership of these organisations does not necessarily mean that they are 'perfect' estate agents, but it does mean that there are certain standards they must adhere to, in order to be members of any of these professional bodies. I have to admit to using an estate agent once, for letting purposes, who was not registered with any of these professional bodies, but who was personally recommended, and it was not a success. I will go into what happened in the section on ugly estate agents.

TIP

Never forget that an estate agent works on commission and it is their job to either sell or rent the property for you, as quickly as they can. The selling of a property, particularly if it is sole representation, is not as competitive as the rental market, where all the agents are competing for the same business. The property can be registered with several agents at once, with no increase in commission charges. Only let an estate agent know what you want them to know. If you confide to them that you will take a reduced asking price or a reduced rent, then that is what you will probably end up with. Be flexible but don't talk about specific reductions. It's up to the agent to get offers and it is up to you whether you accept them or not.

SELLING YOUR PROPERTY

The first step on the roller coaster of selling your property will be to employ an estate agent. Or, if you decide to sell your property privately, you will need to decide on the price you want and take out the necessary advertising in the newspapers or on the Internet. If you appoint an estate agent it will be their job to value your property and my advice is to get at least three valuations.

Valuations

Do not necessarily choose the agent who gives the highest valuation, as it is important to remember that they want to lure you into an exclusive 'sole agency' agreement. They may well give you a high valuation in order to secure the contract, and it is common for estate agents who give high valuations to lower the asking price after a couple of weeks, or come in with offers well below the asking price. It is important that you research the market yourself, to get an idea of what is an appropriate price for your property.

- Get three valuations.
- Ask to see terms and conditions.
- Ask what advertising methods the agent employs.
- Check what their commission rate is.
- Choose a local estate agent (they will know the local market).
- After agreeing which agent you are choosing, enter a 'sole agency agreement', as this will save on commission.

TIP

If you are going 'sole agency', set a time limit on it (six weeks) and have this written into your agreement. If you are not satisfied with the agent's efforts after the agreed contract time expires, you can try another agent and enter another 'sole agency' agreement, without incurring multiple agency charges (which can be significantly higher).

Commission

The commission rate can vary from agency to agency and from area to area. It can be anything between 1% and 4%. If the commission rate is high, negotiate it down. I have always negotiated on commission charges and although the reduction may only be 0.5% it is worth having, as the commission charges can stack up on an expensive property. Even if the property is not expensive, it's still worth negotiating on the commission. Make sure any reductions are put in writing!

Property description

Once you have instructed the agent, they will draw up the property details. Ask to see a copy of this before the property is marketed and if you think you can add any useful suggestions to the description, or the property is not being accurately described, don't be afraid to put your ideas forward. Remember, however, that an agent's description may not always be perfect but generally, they will know how to describe a property better than you can and highlight the selling points. They will also know the limitations of their advertising space. Remember, it is an estate agent's job to sell your property and they are likely to describe your property in the most flattering terms. I remember a property being described as having a paved garden area, only to discover it had only a small slab of concrete outside the back door!

Advertising

It is an agent's job to advertise your property in newspapers, property journals and on their website. Marketing is the area which costs the agent a great deal of money and does not always result in either a sale or a rental. Advertising space is a necessary expense, as it is the agent's job to sell or rent the property as soon as possible and to do that they need to appeal to as wide a market as they can. It is also an estate agent's job to provide good property details, preferably including colour pictures.

TIP

If you are undecided about an agent, ask to see examples of their property details. Do they look well presented? Check to see what papers they advertise in and buy copies to see how they present the properties and what size their advertising space is. If they have a website (and it is my view that they all should) then look it up on the Internet. Ask how often it is updated. Check out other agent's websites and compare them. This is a good way of comparing property prices too! A useful website to find estate agents in a chosen area is: www.yell.com.

GOOD LETTING AGENTS

If you are choosing to rent out your property, rather than sell it, you will need the services of a letting agent. If, however, you decide to rent out the property privately, this will save you on fees but what you save on fees, could cost you on headaches. So, before going ahead with any private let, make sure you know what will be expected of you, if you are to secure a 'happy' tenancy. My own advice is to always use a reputable letting agent who is a member of a professional body.

How much does a letting agent charge?

This can vary but a general rule for the letting service is between 8% and 10%.

What a letting agent does for their fee

Terms and conditions vary from agent to agent but if they are a member of a professional body, they should offer a certain standard of service. For example, a good agent should be able to offer:

- proactive marketing
- sourcing of tenants from an active 'would be' tenant database
- advertising on a constantly updated website
- high quality property details
- regular feedback on property viewing
- the best rental price in a short time

What happens when they have found a tenant?

You will have to decide what kind of letting service you require. If you want a let only service, as opposed to a full management service, then the service the estate agent provides will be something on the lines of:

- Introduction of prospective tenant, negotiating terms and conditions between you.

- Reference checks.

- Collect and hold the deposit (as stakeholders) against arrears and dilapidations.

- Arrange to have the deposit repaid to the tenant at the end of the tenancy, subject to any dilapidation costs or arrears and subject to agreement between the two parties regarding the inventory report.

Arranging the inventory

If you opt for the 'let only' service, it will be your job to organise getting an inventory done. Ask your estate agent to recommend an inventory clerk.

When do I pay the letting fee?

Most agents will take this payment in advance and it will be a percentage of all rent payable during the full tenancy agreement. In real terms, it means that until all the commission has been deducted, you will not get any money! Should the tenant break the agreement, for any reason, you will get a refund on the advance lettings fee paid to the agent. It is important when you are doing your budget that you factor in that the first month's rent will probably go on commission.

Letting and rent collection

An average charge for this service is 12.5%. This will involve all of the above and if not already included in that service, an arrangement to collect the rent and pay it directly to you. This extra 12.5% is deducted monthly from the rental payment.

Full management service

Full management service does not come cheap and can cost an extra 2% to 6% on top of the letting fee. This is a considerable chunk out of any rental income and can have an adverse effect on your property's rental return. I choose to have my properties professionally managed because I do not have the time and, to be honest, the inclination to be permanently on call. If something goes wrong and the tenant wants it fixed quickly, I may not be in the best position to do that. I would rather leave that aspect of being a landlady to the professionals, who should have a database of tradespeople that they use should any problems occur. At the same time, I would always keep an eye on any expenses and if a charge seemed steep, I would obviously question it.

What does a full management service provide?

This is a comprehensive service and saves you having to be on call yourself. If you have just one property and it is close to where you live, then by all means manage it yourself and save yourself the extra commission. If you have a portfolio of properties or are wishing to concentrate your energies on achieving that, I would suggest getting the properties professionally managed – if only to save on the headaches! Some large corporate companies will only agree to rent a property if it is professionally managed. This also applies to some relocation agents.

The extra percentage for full management will be deducted monthly or when the rent is paid. The service will include:

- Agreeing terms and conditions between the landlord and the tenant.
- Taking up references.

- Organising a gas safety report.
- Organising an electrical safety report.
- Drawing up the tenancy agreement (which will incur an additional charge of approximately £75–£150).
- Arranging an inventory clerk.
- Checking the tenant in.
- Organising the property to be professionally cleaned.
- Collecting and holding the deposit (as stakeholders).
- Rent collection.
- Repairs and replacements.
- Property visits (these can be added at an additional charge).
- Renewals.
- Arranging an inventory check out report.
- Checking out the tenant.
- Payment of utility bills, ground rent, service charge, council tax out of rental received.
- Notification to utility companies and council of change of tenancy.

TIP

Even though I have my properties professionally managed, I have a standard letter that I send out to the relevant local authority regarding council tax. I have in the past received council tax demands that the tenant should have paid, only to find out that the local authority had not been informed of the tenancy in the first place. It is far simpler to leave a paper trail with the local authority yourself, regarding who is living in the property and when the tenancy started, than to leave it to an agent, no matter how reputable!

Costs you will still be responsible for
- VAT on commissions, fees and charges.
- Building/contents insurance.
- Ground rent.

- Service charges.
- Council tax (when the property is empty) and payable at the 'empty' rate.
- Utility bills (when the property is empty).
- Maintenance charges.
- The gas/electric safety certificates.
- The inventory.

The inventory

Most letting agents will be able to provide you with this service. The cost will be dependent on the size of the property and whether it is furnished or not. The cost of an inventory for a standard two bedroom flat can vary from £75 to £150.

TIP

Some estate agents have written into their terms and conditions that it is the landlord's responsibility to pay for the check in and the tenant's responsibility to pay for the check out. Check the terms and conditions to see whether this is included and if it isn't, ask if it can be, especially if you are getting a below market value rent.

What exactly is an inventory?

An inventory should be an in-depth document, not only listing all items that are in the apartment but also what condition they are in. It will also comment on the décor of each room and whether it is decorated to a good standard. It will cover whether the property is clean or not, if the carpets have been cleaned and the curtains dry cleaned. An inventory clerk will also read the meters at the beginning and end of the tenancy. A good inventory will cover everything, even the chip in the tile above the bath!

Can I do the inventory myself?

Yes, but I would not advise it. If you do the inventory yourself and something gets damaged, you will have difficulty in getting replacement costs if the tenant disputes it. Having an independent inventory should make that task easier, particularly if the same inventory clerk also does the check out. Most estate agents have reputable independent inventory clerks that they use regularly and should know the good ones from the bad.

TIP

If you wish to instruct an inventory clerk independently, ask to see a sample of a recent inventory that they have taken and compare this with other samples. As a rule of thumb, the one to go for is the one with most detail!

Dilapidations deposit

The dilapidations deposit is generally held by the letting agent as a stakeholder. This will be paid back to the tenant at the end of the tenancy, when the inventory has been agreed. The dilapidation deposit is generally about four to six weeks' rent in advance.

TIP

Some agents will suggest taking only a four week dilapidation deposit and this can be at the request of the tenant. My advice is to always ask for a minimum of at least six weeks' deposit, as in my experience, I have found that a lot of tenants tend not to pay the last month's rent! If all the deposit is taken up in rent arrears, this will leave nothing in the 'pot' for dilapidations, cleaning or unpaid bills.

Unpaid bills

I once had a tenant who, after ending the tenancy, left the apartment with a £400 electricity bill hanging over its head. Whilst it is not the landlord's responsibility to pay this bill, it does tend to cause complications when the next account needs to be opened. If outstanding bills are constantly a problem for the utility companies at a particular property, they may demand that a deposit is paid in advance before they agree to take out a new contract and this might put a tenant off. Fortunately, in my case, there was enough in the deposit to pay off the rather large electricity bill.

TIP

If an agent is managing your property and it is stated in their terms and conditions that they will inform the utility companies and local council of the end of the tenancy, ask for copies of letters sent. These will be useful for your files (should any discrepancy arise) but more importantly, they will be proof that the agents have done the job they agreed to do in their terms and conditions. If not, you could end up with a surplus bill, still registered in the old tenant's name, and this may be difficult, even in view of the inventory, to resolve. This has happened to me before and I have learnt from my experiences that no matter how reputable the agent, this part of the service they offer is often lacking.

Other matters

- **The landlord consent to data being processed**, i.e. information and personal details on or of the landlord as defined in the Data Protection Act 1988.

- **Rents received**. There will be a clearing process (up to ten days) of rents received to the agent, before being transferred into the client's account.

- **Instructions to solicitors**. Should there be a problem with rent arrears or any other dispute with the tenant that involves litigation, the legal costs incurred will be the landlord's responsibility.

- **Renewals**. If a tenant wishes to renew the tenancy for a further term, then commissions will still be payable to the agent, who will renegotiate on your behalf.

- **Insurance claims**. These will generally incur an extra cost payable to the agent for any work undertaken on your behalf, with regards to making a claim.

- **Work to properties**. If an agent is to be present for any works being carried out at the property, this will generally incur an extra charge by them.

- **Purchase**. Should the tenant wish to purchase the property, commission on the sale of the property will be payable to the agent as agreed in the terms and conditions.

- **Interest on monies held**. Any deposits or working funds held by the letting agent will benefit from interest accrued. Check terms and conditions to see who will benefit from this interest (it is unlikely to be you!).

- **Cancellation fee**. You may have to pay a cancellation fee if, for whatever reason, you are unable to go ahead with the tenancy after terms and conditions have been agreed by both parties.

- **Certificate of ownership**. You will have to sign documentation that you own the property and are a UK resident. You may be required to provide the Land Registry Title Number and proof of ownership if you are a company or trust.

- **Vacant management service**. If the property is vacant between tenancies, some agents will offer a service which will mean regular inspections and attention to any maintenance issues which may occur. There will be an additional fee for this service.

The Taxes Act 1988 and the Taxation of Income from Land (non-residents) Regulations of 1995

It will be your responsibility to notify the Inland Revenue of the tenancy. If you live abroad, the Inland Revenue will hold the agent responsible for the payment of any tax liability on rents collected on your behalf, unless an Approval Certificate is provided. Accordingly, any rent collected on your behalf by the agent will have deductions made for taxes, which will be held in an account until an Approval Certificate is provided or the monies are forwarded to the Inland Revenue (on a quarterly basis). Should the tax withheld be less than the amount forwarded to the tax authorities by the agent, it will be the landlord's responsibility to liase directly with the Inspector of Taxes regarding a refund.

Taxes Management Act 1970

The agent is legally responsible for disclosing the following information to the Inland Revenue on an annual basis and this includes all resident UK landlords as well as overseas landlords:

+ Name and address of the landlord.
+ Address of the property being let.
+ Amount of income collected on behalf of the landlord.
+ The relevant tax year that monies relate to.
+ The source of the income.

BAD ESTATE AGENTS

There has been a 25% rise in complaints about estate agents over the last year. There have been calls for estate agents to be trained, face greater statutory regulations and for them to join an independent ombudsman scheme, which would arbitrate, should any disputes arise between estate agent and client. Out of the UK's 12,000 estate agents only 36% belong to an ombudsman scheme, which not only investigates complaints from clients but also bad practices between rival estate agents.

Common complaints

◆ The most common complaint from vendors was that estate agents sometimes failed to pass on relevant offers. This was because the estate agent had an undeclared vested interest in the property and wanted to keep the offers from the vendor, so that they could later secure the property for either themselves, or other interested parties, at below market value.

◆ Another complaint was that clients were not allowed to view properties unless they agreed to purchase a mortgage from the estate agent.

◆ Another was 'flyboarding' – a practice where 'ugly' agents stick 'for sale' boards up at random, even if there is no property to sell.

TIP

It is important when choosing to sell your property through an estate agent that you have an idea of what the property is worth. You can do this by looking in local estate agents' windows to compare prices, reading the local property papers and, of course, getting more than one valuation.

UGLY ESTATE AGENTS AND LETTING AGENTS

I have only come across one really 'ugly' estate agent but I know that there are many more out there. The estate agent I used was new to the area and had been recommended to me by a friend. She was not a member of any professional body but because of the personal recommendation I, foolishly, did not concern myself with that too much.

I had a new apartment in London's Docklands that was released at the same time as many other apartments in the block. It was also in 'Phase 1', which meant that the rest of the block was still a building site, making the apartment difficult to rent out. The rental market was slow and in order to get myself a tenant, I was prepared to cast my net wider than I had done in the past, and use agents that I had not used before.

What happened

♦ **Alarm Bell 1**. The 'ugly' estate agent managed to find me a tenant the day after the instruction. Alarm bells should have rung then, as none of the established agents in the area had been able to find me a tenant. However, I was so keen to end the void period that I didn't allow myself to have any doubts about the situation.

♦ **Alarm Bell 2**. The estate agent informed me that her tenant wanted to move in the next day. I did find this odd but the estate agent assured me that her tenant was a respectable businessman, who wanted the apartment to house employees from his holiday vacation company. She also informed me she was currently renting out two other properties to him, that she had never had any problems with him in the past and that he was an ideal tenant.

♦ **Alarm Bell 3**. I went to meet the agent the following day to sign the tenancy agreement. I was suspicious about her manner, which seemed a little shifty, but as I had not met her before, I had nothing tangible to go on and put this down to her personality.

♦ **Alarm Bell 4**. The tenancy agreement did not have a six months break clause. The prospective tenant wanted it for the full 12 months. I questioned this, as he had not even seen the property. The agent assured me that would not be necessary, as the agents had inspected it and that this particular tenant always went along with their recommendations. As this was a high spec apartment and beautifully furnished I had no problem believing that. However, I was not happy to sign the contract without a break clause and this is what eventually saved the day!

◆ **Alarm Bell 5**. The references which she assured me were valid appeared to be vague.

The scam

Fortunately, because I did not sign the contract, I was saved from having a horrendous tenant living in my beautiful apartment. The tenant in question was running a sub-letting business to holiday-makers, innocents from abroad and multiple students (as many as 13), in two-bedroom apartments. He was promising them serviced apartments, charging them by the night and then not paying the landlord anything! He had countless County Court judgements against him and was not afraid of the law. He knew he could use the apartments for at least six months without paying any rent and that it would be up to the landlord to take out expensive legal action against him, to regain possession of their flat. He was well versed in English law and had built a large business by robbing landlords of their rent and 'holiday-makers' of their money. He would make no effort to restore the apartments after they had been misused and over-populated (effectively trashed). He operates not only in London but also in Paris. The ugly agent was fully aware of the situation and knowingly led me into it. When I tried to question her about events she did not answer her phone or indeed go into work. Her business partner was also unavailable for comment, as he had suddenly taken an unexpected holiday!

If you hear an alarm bell – no matter how desperate you may be to find a tenant
for your property – listen to it!

SUMMARY

Make a friend of your estate agent. If you are in the property
business, you need contacts that will help you secure properties to
buy. Remember, you are always looking for properties below
market value, in order to maximise your 'property profit
potential'. You will also need agents to find you the best tenants
and do the most stringent tests to avoid tenant nasties.

If an estate agent has set up overnight, be wary, as they will be
running high business costs and they will be operating in a very
competitive market, so some of them will cut corners in order to
secure a deal. If you have any doubts at all about an agent then
chose one with a track record.

I have estate agents that I use over and over again – they know I
am a serious investor and I know that they are agents I can trust.
Remember, relationships are not built up overnight and it will
take time to sort out the good from the bad.

As virtually anyone can set themselves up as an estate agent, you
need to be wary at all times and safeguard yourself from the 'ugly'
ones who don't care about you, or your returning business, but
care only about sharp deals and a fast buck. The best way of
doing this is to only choose agents who are members of a
professional body! I am sorry for banging on about this, but it is
vital if you don't want to be eaten by sharks!

9

Holiday Lets and Second Homes

If you are looking for a second home, not only for fun but also as an investment, then letting it out as a holiday home may be something you wish to consider. There are several tax advantages to owning a holiday home that you are renting out and these tax incentives may make the proposition of owning a second home financially viable for you. Holiday accommodation not only offers the opportunity of 'holidays on tap', it is also another way of getting someone else to pay the mortgage for you, whilst the property appreciates in value. There are also capital gains tax advantages to owning a property designated as a holiday home (see Chapter 6).

WHAT IS A HOLIDAY LET?
The 1996 Housing Act definition of a holiday let is 'a let to a person or group of people, where the purpose of the occupation is that of a holiday'. Any person over the age of 16 who pays to sleep in your property must be registered with you. This means supplying you with their full name (and passport details if applicable) and a forwarding address. If you use a professional holiday letting company they will do this for you.

LOCATION
As with all property, the location of your holiday home will be an important consideration from a rental point of view. If you want to own a holiday home, then it is likely you will want it to be in an area that has some tourist appeal, otherwise presumably, you

would not want to holiday there! Where you choose to invest in your holiday home will obviously be a personal choice, which may be governed by several non-commercial factors such as being close to family, friends, etc. If you choose to invest in a second home purely for personal use, it would be prudent to remember that some day you may want to sell the property.

Remote areas

If the area you want to buy in is totally remote and a considerable distance from any attractions, it may not have great re-sale prospects. In other words, your target market will be very small, both for rental and re-sale, so consider very carefully exactly what the primary purpose of owning a second home is for you, before you purchase. If you are serious about being a property millionaire, your primary purpose will always be the ability to maximise on the 'property profit potential' but that does not mean to say you can't have fun, as long as you make informed choices.

Ideal locations

- ◆ Near major tourist attractions.
- ◆ Beauty spots.
- ◆ Near the coast.
- ◆ Close to areas of historical interest.
- ◆ Close to areas of architectural interest.

WHAT TYPE OF HOLIDAY ACCOMMODATION IS MOST SUITABLE FOR LETTING?

The general preference is for cottage type accommodation which can sleep four to six. Obviously, the more your property sleeps, the wider your market will be. My own holiday cottage sleeps six and I would not advise buying anything bigger than this. Larger

properties that sleep more will put a lot more wear and tear on
your appliances and perhaps make accidents and breakages more
likely to happen. I prefer a limited number of holiday guests, as
this makes changeovers more manageable.

USING A HOLIDAY LETTING COMPANY

It is the job of a holiday letting company to obtain clients on your
behalf. If the holiday letting company is established, it will no
doubt produce a colour brochure each year, advertising the
properties it has registered with them. It will send these brochures
out, not only to new clients but also to its existing client database.

New clients will be generated from sources such as advertising
campaigns in magazines, guide-books and more importantly these
days, the Internet. The website of any holiday letting company
should show a full range of properties, searchable by location, size
and price and should invite enquiries by e-mail. If you are
thinking of using the services of one of these companies, check
out their website first, to see if you like the presentation.

Holiday letting companies – the personal approach

Some holiday letting companies guarantee to vet all their
properties personally. This can be reassuring not only for the
client but also for you, as you will have a personal contact with a
company employee who is working on your behalf. I like to use a
holiday company that uses this approach, as they generally speak
to their clients directly and this can help to avoid confusion over
bookings. Also, if they have visited the property personally, they
will be able to offer a genuine recommendation and be able to
match clients' needs from first-hand experience.

How does it work?

Bookings are accepted in accordance with the terms and conditions set out by the individual holiday company. Some companies offer a full management service that will take care of all aspects of running the holiday let business for you. Expect to pay a considerable amount for this, in the region of 40–50% of the anticipated holiday rental, as this will not only have to cover agency fees but also all the caretaker expenses. Other companies operate more as an agent and will generally charge 20% of the holiday rental, plus VAT. It will be their job to offer out your property and to take bookings on your behalf.

Bookings through a holiday company

Bookings are accepted in accordance with the agreement between the owner and the holiday company. All bookings should be confirmed, in writing, to you and the client, once the client's deposit payment has been received. Full payment of the rent due, plus details of the booking, will be sent to owners two to three weeks before the start of each holiday, together with, if possible, the clients' anticipated arrival time. Clients will be sent details of the property, comprehensive directions and detailed arrangements for key collection. Telephone numbers of owners/caretakers are provided with this package, to enable clients to communicate any last minute change of arrival times or unexpected delays. This procedure could differ slightly depending on which holiday company you choose to use.

TIP

Arrivals late in the evening are not uncommon and if someone is likely to arrive late and your caretaker is not available, you may want to leave the key with someone that you can trust. It is worth talking to the landlord/lady of the nearest local pub, to see if you can arrange for a set of keys to be left there. They may want a small fee for this service or they may be happy to do this as they will realise that your guests are likely to be customers of the pub for the duration of their holiday – particularly if they receive a warm welcome at the local! My own holiday cottage is situated almost next door to a pub, so this arrangement works well for me.

Cancellation insurance

Most holiday companies will offer cancellation insurance. This enables clients to get some, if not all, of their money back in the unhappy event that they have to cancel their holiday. If the agency works in conjunction with other agencies in the EU, the regulations may differ slightly but offer much the same benefits. It is becoming increasingly common that customers have their own annual travel insurance policies. It is up to the holiday company to check that the cover provided is adequate and if it is not they should inform clients of their obligations to pay the rent in full, if they have to cancel and the property cannot be re-let.

Property insurance

Most domestic buildings and contents insurance policies do not provide cover when the property is used for holiday lettings and they certainly do not provide cover for the loss of income should your property need to be repaired, is inaccessible or otherwise out of use. Most holiday companies will have contacts with specialist insurers who deal with issues relating to holiday lets. Ask your holiday company for their details.

TIP

Even though I employ the services of both a holiday company and a caretaker, I always ask for a copy of the booking form to be sent directly to me. I stick my booking forms into my holiday cottage diary, which I keep up to date and in a safe place. I also make a copy of these bookings onto a calendar in case (woe of woes) my holiday diary should go missing. Not only will this allow you to know who is staying in your property but will also allow you to keep an eye out for any window of opportunity to use the property yourself. It will also be necessary for tax purposes to have an up-to-date diary of bookings with visitors details and you will need to keep these for a minimum of 12 months.

ACCOMMODATION QUALITY ASSESSMENT

Hotel and guest accommodation proprietors can choose to have their establishments assessed by one of the three national organisations, in order to receive either a star rating (hotels) or a diamond rating (guest accommodation). The English Tourism Council, the AA and the RAC all offer this service, which involves the completion by you of an assessment application form and payment of a fee (dependent on the size of the property). An assessor will then visit your property to establish the number of stars/diamonds that you are eligible for.

TIP

If you are going to be running your holiday letting business yourself this will be a useful rating to include in your brochure.

If you are using an established holiday company this may not be as necessary, as a representative of the company will have visited your property and made their own assessment which they will base their advertising on. Most companies that do their own assessment should be members of EASCO, the English Association of Self Catering Operators. Check with the holiday company that they are registered with this authority. Other authorities are:

- ASSC, the Association of Scotland's Self Caterers
- WASCO, the Wales Association of Self Catering Operators
- NISCHA, the Northern Ireland Self Catering Holiday Association.

FIRE SAFETY

Contact your local Fire Brigade Safety Officer to check that you comply with fire precaution requirements. Broadly, these apply to any property capable of sleeping over six people (excluding yourself and your family) including any employee and any property sleeping six or less, where any person sleeps either at basement level or above first floor level.

THE DIY APPROACH TO HOLIDAY LETTING

If you have the time and do not mind answering the phone and doing your own paperwork, you may choose not to use the services of a holiday letting company and save yourself their commission fees. The arrival of the Internet has made this easier, as you can set up your own web page advertising your property. You will, however, need to have a brochure printed about your property, as you will have to send this out to prospective customers.

The brochure/flyer

This should contain comprehensive and accurate details about your property. It is the property you are trying to sell to your clients, not necessarily the area, as they will most probably have decided on where they want to holiday before they approach you.

Be accurate with your property description

Do not make claims in your brochure that are not accurate, as you do not want a disgruntled holidaymaker who has had their holiday ruined because of your claims. If the rooms are small, then do not say they are big; if the property is not close to local amenities, don't say it is. The holidaymaker will have a right to demand their money back if you have sent them misleading information.

TIP

When designing your brochure/flyer, always print your seasonal rates on a separate piece of paper and include this with your brochure. The reason for this is that your rates will change from year to year and you do not want the expense of reprinting your brochure annually!

Setting the weekly rate

Check with your local tourist board what the rates are for properties in the area similar to yours and take into account seasonal variations. The rates you charge will have no effect on the classification and grading.

Bookings

Always ask for a non-returnable reservation fee. This should be 25% of the holiday rental. Once you have received this and you have cleared funds in your bank account, you can then send the client a confirmation of the booking. With this confirmation, you will need to send an invoice for the balance due. Confirm that you will need this to be paid in full, 28 days before the holiday is due to commence. If payment is not received by this date, you will be entitled to keep the reservation deposit as a cancellation fee.

> **TIP**
>
> People can sometimes forget, quite genuinely, to pay the balance on the agreed date. A gentle reminder by phone is sometimes all that is needed. If the balance still fails to arrive, you can speak to the client again and ask them to send you the remittance by return, otherwise you will have to remarket the property.

When the balance is received

When sending the receipt, inform the client of the key collection arrangements and the time that they can enter the property. If you have agreed to charge for certain extras and have arranged for a damage deposit to be paid, always ask for these to be paid in cash on arrival. This saves funds having to be cleared and in the event of a cancellation, funds having to be returned.

Cancellations

You will need to set out your requirements for this in your terms and conditions, which will be included in your brochure. It is important that you state in all your documentation exactly what your terms and conditions are. This can be done as a simple footer on the bottom of all receipts, invoices, etc. It is inevitable that cancellations will happen from time to time but it is unusual for these to happen after the full balance has been paid. If this does happen, it will generally be for an insurable reason, in which case, you should not find yourself out of funds.

> **TIP**
>
> It is always a good idea to make holiday insurance a necessity of the booking conditions. You can include this in your terms and conditions.

How long is the holiday season?

The holiday season, in the right property, in the right location, can be almost all year round. This may not involve the property being let all the time at the peak summer rate but it could involve long weekend breaks, which are becoming more and more popular. Christmas/New Year, Easter and the Spring Bank Holiday weekend, although technically out of season, are all popular times for letting and, as such, generally carry a price premium.

♦ Low season – January, February, March.
♦ Mid season – April, May, June, September, October, November December.
♦ High season – July and August.

What extras can I charge for?

♦ During the low and mid season, you can add a heating surcharge but this must be agreed with the guest at the time of booking.
♦ If pets are allowed by arrangement, you may add an additional charge, again to be agreed at the time of booking.
♦ Towel hire (if these are not included).
♦ Linen hire (if not included).
♦ Babysitting services (if you are able to offer this).

TIP

Try to keep any extra charges to a minimum. I always include linen in my weekly charge but not towels. I charge a small sum for towels, as the laundering of these involves extra work for the caretaker. It certainly is more convenient if guests bring their own, as towels take a considerable amount of drying time. If you are going to provide towels and your holiday home is situated near a coastal resort, consider providing beach towels, as this is inevitably where they will end up!

Council tax/water rates and utility bills

You will be responsible for paying these bills in the usual way. Until recently, second homeowners were given considerable discounts on their council tax. This has now changed and some local councils will only offer a 10% discount.

CARETAKERS/KEY HOLDERS

This is the most difficult area to get right when letting out a holiday cottage and it is important (if you are not available to do this yourself or don't want to do it) that you employ a trustworthy and reliable caretaker for the property. Finding these 'diamonds' is not always easy but if you do find one, make sure you nurture your relationship with them. The caretaker will be the first point of contact your guests will have when they arrive at the property.

What are the duties of a caretaker/key holder?

It will be the caretaker's job to hold the keys to the property. As such, they will be expected to meet and greet the guests on their arrival. It will be their job to settle the guests into the house and explain whatever they need to know about how the house functions, such as the heating, etc. If your guests have had a long journey to the property, the friendliness of this greeting will be all important and will hopefully help them to get the best out of their holiday.

CHANGEOVERS

The changeover is when one set of visitors leaves and another set is due to arrive. The departure time is usually **10am** and the arrival time after **2.30pm.** The time in between is used for the changeover, which involves:

- changeover of linen
- full clean of property
- minor repairs, such as change of light bulbs, etc.
- providing towels (if hired)
- erecting cot (if hired)
- cleaning windows
- gardening duties (if applicable)
- if any breakages, sorting out replacements.

The caretaker will be very busy during the changeover period, as it is important that everything is in place before the next visitors are due to arrive. This will include stripping the beds, emptying the fridge of all perishables and most importantly of all, making sure the place is spotlessly clean.

Arrival checklist
- Make sure the keys are all present and correct and in full working order.

- Either you or your caretaker should be available to show your visitor around.

- Show the visitor how to switch the heating and hot water on.

- Collect any deposits for keys, heating or breakages.

- Leave the property inventory and instruction manuals clearly visible.

- Remind them that they need to vacate the property at the agreed departure time. If they have to leave at any other time, they will need to discuss this with you so that arrangements can be made for the key collection.

- If your guest is an overseas visitor and has difficulty understanding the language, take time to explain everything clearly and make sure that they have your number handy, so that they contact you if there are any problems.

- Don't forget to provide a fire extinguisher and leave it clearly visible.

TIP

If the property is well presented and is not full of Granny's cast-offs, the chances are that your guests will do their best to keep the property in good order too. If the furnishings are tatty and the plates are chipped then you have only got yourself to blame if the property is left in a mess!

WHAT WRITTEN INFORMATION SHOULD I LEAVE ABOUT THE PROPERTY?

- Your own and/or your local key holder's phone numbers for emergencies.

- Where to find: spare lamp bulbs; emergency lighting i.e. torches; meters, fuse box and earth trip switch; water stop cock.

- Notes on refuse collection day and where to put it for collection.

- Inventory/help lists.

Help lists

For the convenience of your guests, leave help lists over the appliances. This will save them having to plough through complicated instruction manuals and it will also hopefully reduce the chance of damage to your appliances through misuse. It is advisable to leave help lists over such things as:

- washing machine
- dishwasher
- tumble-dryer
- oven
- microwave
- heating and hot water system
- TV/video/stereo/DVD player.

Useful information about the area
- Local accident and emergency hospital
- Doctor
- Vet (if animals are accepted in your property)
- Nearest pay-phone
- Local shops for milk, newspapers and groceries (with opening times if possible)
- Pubs, wine bars, restaurants, takeaways
- Supermarket
- Churches (various religions)
- Information/leaflets on local places of interest
- Nearest public transport
- Taxi firms
- Local maps with details of footpaths, walks, cycle routes, etc.

TIP

Leave your visitor with a comprehensive list of what the area has to offer and present all this neatly in a folder to be left in the property. This will not only help your guests get the most out of their stay, it will also encourage them to come back again. Remember, repeat business is the life and soul of holiday letting!

WHAT DO I NEED TO PROVIDE IN THE WAY OF FURNISHINGS?

With standard letting, a property needs to provide the basics but very little else, as the tenant will no doubt have things of their own that they will like to add. Most of these tenancies are for period of six months to a year and, as such, the long stay tenant will be treating their rented accommodation as their home. They certainly will not want it cluttered with the landlord's ornaments and 'knick-knacks'.

With a holiday let, however, you will not be catering for tenants but for visitors/guests to your home. Most will be staying a week to two weeks and a few home comforts will be most welcomed. This does not mean to say that you want to clutter the property, as not only will this make it difficult to clean, it will also increase your risk of damages. Items that you could consider including would be:

- pictures (particularly nice if they appertain to the area)
- books and magazines
- videos (to keep the kids amused on those inevitable rainy days)
- ornaments (but nothing too fragile)
- board games/cards
- potted plants
- a visitors book.

OUT OF SEASON TENANCIES

If you are not intending to use your property out of season and are not considering letting it out for short lets, you may want to consider a 'long let'. In order for your property to still qualify as a holiday home, the property must have been rented out on a holiday basis before any 'long lets' can be considered. You can recover possession of any 'long let', provided you serve the statutory notice on your tenant (prior to the tenancy commencing) that the tenancy is an 'out of season tenancy'. If you fail to do this, your tenant will have the right to stay for a minimum of six months before you can take any action to regain possession.

VISITORS WITH DISABILITIES

Disability does not necessarily concern only wheelchair access and there are many things that should be done and could be done to help people who are disabled in any way. Visit the Disability Discrimination Act website at www.drc.org.uk/whatwedo/ guestacom.asp for up-to-date guidelines and regulations.

EQUIPMENT LIST (ESSENTIALS)

General
◆ Spare keys
◆ Dustbin
◆ Smoke detectors
◆ Clothes drying facilities
◆ Iron and ironing board
◆ Vacuum cleaner
◆ Broom, mop/bucket, duster, dustpan/brush
◆ Cleaning agents
◆ Suitable hooks for outdoor clothing
◆ Door mat(s)
◆ Non-flammable waste bins
◆ Spare amp bulbs and fuses if appropriate
◆ Curtains/blinds to all windows if overlooked

Kitchen
◆ Adequate work surfaces and cupboard space
◆ Cooker with rings, oven and grill
◆ Microwave

- Toaster and toast rack
- Fridge/freezer (or at least with a freezer compartment)
- Washing up bowl and brush
- Dish drying rack
- Hooks for cloths/towels
- Fire extinguisher or blanket
- Bread bin, bread board, chopping board
- Electric kettle
- Saucepans, frying pan
- Casserole dishes
- Baking tray
- Mixing bowl, colander
- Oven cloth/mitts
- Cutlery, assorted knives, grater, peeler, scissors, ladle, fish slice, wooden spoon, egg cups, butter dish, condiment set
- Crockery to include dinner plates, cereal bowls, small plates, mugs, vegetable dishes, milk jug, sugar bowl
- Salad bowl
- Table mats, coasters, trays
- Glass tumblers, wine glasses, water jug
- Cutlery (in generous quantities)

Sitting room
- Comfortable seating for at least the number of people accommodated
- Storage for bedding and guests' clothes, if a sofa bed is provided
- Coffee table/occasional table
- Dining table and chairs
- Colour TV
- Lamps

Bathrooms
- Lock or bolt on door

- Mirror, shelf or cabinet
- Towel rail/clothes hook
- Bath/shower mat
- Toilet roll holder and toilet paper
- Toilet brush
- Lidded bin
- Opening window/extractor fan
- Shaver point

Bedrooms

- Double beds
- Single beds (adult size)
- All beds to have: mattress protector, two pillows per person, duvet, blankets, duvet covers (not nylon!)
- Adequate hanging space with ample coat hangers (not wire)
- Drawers and or shelf space
- Bedside carpet, rugs, lamps, bedside tables
- Mirror, chair or stool and waste bin

Garden/outdoor area

- Suitable access lighting
- Garden furniture, as appropriate

Don't forget

- All equipment must be of suitable size and a generous quantity for the numbers provided.
- All upholstered furnishings must comply with current fire regulations.
- All gas and electric equipment must be covered by current safety certificates. These must be checked annually.

IS THERE A DOWNSIDE TO HOLIDAY LETTING?

The biggest drawback with holiday lets is that you will most likely not be able to use your property when you would like. High season is the most popular time and that is when you will be able to charge a premium for your property. If you want to use it during the summer months this will not only be uneconomical but will also jeopardise your relationship with your holiday company (if you choose to use one), as they will not want to spend money advertising the property if is not available at peak times.

This does not mean that you can't use your property at all during the popular months, it just means you will have to be reasonable with your requests. You will also have to book your own time, as the holiday company will need to know when you intend to use the property yourself, in order to avoid double bookings.

SUMMARY

Holiday lets differ from standard lets, as your guests' expectations will be higher. They will have considered at great length where to go for their holiday and where to stay, and will probably have booked their holiday accommodation well in advance. It is important that when they arrive everything is clean and welcoming. You would hate to be responsible for ruining someone's hard-earned holiday!

Buying in Spain

Having a second home in Spain is becoming a must for Britons in search of a place in the sun. The Spanish property market is the most buoyant in Europe and in some publications is described as 'the fastest growing property market in the world'. The *Economist* reports that house prices in Spain have risen faster in the last 20 years than anywhere in the world. In some areas of Spain properties have risen on average over 30% per year.

Experts predict that the Spanish property market will continue to rise, though perhaps not at the same pace as in recent years, and is still a sound investment for those looking to invest overseas. The introduction of the euro has highlighted the fact that Spanish property compares favourably with housing costs in the rest of Europe.

DO YOUR RESEARCH

Anyone wishing to invest in Spain needs to research thoroughly the opportunities offered. There are many new developments and the choice of where to buy and what to buy is vast. This chapter aims to help you make an informed choice and warn you of some of the pitfalls that you may stumble into, resulting in the dream home turning into a nightmare scenario.

It is vital, when considering investing in Spain, that you bear three things in mind:

- You may not speak the language.
- Spanish law is different.
- All that glisters is not gold.

WHY ARE PEOPLE CHOOSING TO INVEST IN SPAIN?

Few developments, soaring UK property prices and the launch of low cost airlines mean that owning a Spanish home, once a luxury that only the rich could afford, is now financially within the means of a much wider market. As traditional investment opportunities continue to offer relatively low returns, more and more people are turning to investing in overseas property. This is not only seen as a sound investment but it can be an enriching lifestyle choice too. The rental opportunities that a Spanish property can provide make it an investment that can contribute substantially towards its funding.

LEGAL AND FINANCIAL ASPECTS

Spanish lawyers

It is advisable to use a Spanish lawyer when purchasing property in Spain, as they will understand the ins and outs of buying in Spain, perhaps more so than a British solicitor who speaks Spanish! It is important that you get sound legal advice before you commit to any purchase. Advise your lawyer that you will require that the contract to be translated into your own language.

TIP

If you want to find out where to contact a good Spanish lawyer, ask advice from people you know. If you do not know of anyone or cannot find any satisfied clients, then contact the British or American Consulate. They can provide you with a list of lawyers in your area who speak English, although they will not officially be allowed to recommend one.

How much are my legal expenses likely to be?

Estimate to pay about 1% of the value of the transaction. Make sure that you have agreed the costs before you instruct your lawyer. Other costs you may be responsible for will be:

- opening of a spanish bank account.
- preparation of spanish identification numbers
- financial advice (both in home country and arrival in Spain)
- arranging a Spanish will
- house contents and building insurance (includes premium payment)
- connection of water and electricity (includes connection fee)
- fiscal representation
- assistance when signing the title deed.

Why do I need a Spanish bank account and a fiscal representative?

You will need a Spanish bank account in order to pay your electricity and water charges by direct debit. A fiscal representative will make payments of your rates at the town hall on your behalf and make sure that your annual property tax is paid.

Do I have to pay for my Spanish property in euros?

You can pay for your property in euros, with a cheque through a Spanish bank account. You can also pay by cheque in a foreign currency. You can also pay by direct transfer from your foreign bank to the vendor's foreign bank.

Can I get a Spanish mortgage?

Mortgages of 100% for periods of 20 and 30 years are now available in Spain. If you are a non-resident purchaser, however, the maximum you will be allowed to borrow will probably be 70% of the property's value. Spanish bank mortgages are currently amongst the lowest in Europe, with rates being offered at less than 5%.

TIP

Always have the facts about the property and exactly what is being included in the asking price carefully checked with your own legal representative. A reputable estate agent who is offering a reputable property for sale will have no objection to you doing this. If there are objections then take that as a warning that all may not be as 'golden' as it is made out to be.

BUYING OFF PLAN IN SPAIN

As in the UK property market, buying off plan offers the opportunity of purchasing at a discount, below market value. As far as investment is concerned and in order to maximise 'property profit potential', you need to invest in the development during the early stages.

How it works

◆ During the construction stage your property rises in value.

◆ The earlier you purchase a property, the greater your discount will be, as the developer will be keen to 'kick start' his development and sell properties below market value.

◆ The market value of each property can be compared with the price of similar properties, with similar specifications, in similar areas.

◆ The more properties a developer sells, the more his financial obligations are met.

◆ The first significant price increases will usually take place in the second phase of the development.

◆ Remaining price increases occur periodically throughout the construction period.

◆ The final phase is generally the most expensive phase.

TIP

If you are intending to sell your investment property in Spain during the construction phase, check with the developer whether you will be allowed to 'on sell', before purchasing the property. If there are restrictions in 'selling the contract on', you will need to look elsewhere and find a development where such practices are allowed.

Inspection trips

Many developers offer 'inspection trips' of the developments they have on offer, which generally last three to four days. The cost of the inspection trips vary and can be anything from £40 upwards. The price includes return flights and a stay in a three star hotel.

Most companies who run such inspection trips claim that they will not use hard sell techniques, but you can be sure that they will do their best to sell you a property before you depart for home. These companies are not out to finance a short break for you in Spain, they are out to sell you a property. That is their business and that is how they make their money. Once you have booked such a trip, they will arrange everything for you, including flights, accommodation and a tour of the area in their air-conditioned mini-buses, to show you the properties on offer. Some companies offer a 'one to one' inspection trip but most will cater for two couples.

TIP

Inspection trips may seem a cheap way of enjoying a few days in Spain but they can turn out to be an expensive mistake, particularly if you leave your common sense at the airport. Three out of four people who go on an inspection trip sign on the dotted line and hand over their reservation fee before their return journey home. If you are tempted to buy, go home first and think it over, rather than get caught up making decisions in the heat of the moment. You may come to regret it later on.

The building plot

On your inspection trip, you will be shown possible building plots that you can choose from. Make sure, when making your choice of plot, that you ask exactly how many properties you will be surrounded by. The plot you are being shown will in all likelihood be in area where there are no immediate dwellings nearby and could well be an empty field. It is important when making your decision that you visualise how the area will look once it is built up. 'Urbanization', as the Spanish like to call it, can involve the building of thousands of villas in one development alone. What could seem like an isolated spot on the inspection trip, could well turn out to be in the midst of a massive housing development, with one villa pretty much on top of another!

If I am shown a building plot that I like, what is the next stage?

In order to secure the plot of your choice, you will generally be asked to hand over a 2,000 euro non-refundable reservation fee. The rest of the payments will be referred to as stage payments. These will vary, depending on which developer you choose to buy from. An average payment scale will be a 40% deposit within 30 days, followed by the final 60%, due on completion. These stage payments will, of course, vary with each development.

The contract price

The contract price should be a fixed price in euros. This will guarantee that should the currency rate alter in relation to sterling (whether the euro goes up or down), the contract price remains the same. To the contract price you will need to add an extra 7% for Spanish IVA, which is the Spanish equivalent of VAT.

TIP

When considering purchasing your off plan property, make sure that your contract states that your payments will be paid into an escrow account, to which the developer has no access, until the property is complete. Most of the reputable developers offer this plan. The bank will repay your money if anything goes wrong.

Will my property be ready within the agreed time scale?

Most developers will give you a completion date of anything from nine months to two years. It would be advisable to consider this date only as a guideline, as the construction process, more often than not, takes longer than anticipated. The developer's agent may well give you a date that is not realistic, in order to get you hooked on buying the property.

I recently visited an agent in Spain who assured me that the completion of most of the villas for sale would be nine to 12 months. When I spoke to people who had actually bought in the development, they advised me that two years was the average most of them had waited before their villa was complete. Some developers may offer compensation should the building plan go over schedule, but this is often difficult to get without an expensive legal wrangle.

What can go wrong?

Some developers may use the stage payment money to complete other properties which were purchased before yours.

Case study

I recently met a couple who had paid 75% of the cost of their villa in stage payments, before a single foundation was laid. This happened because they were based in the UK, and were led to believe that each payment represented another completed stage in the construction of their villa. They decided to make a visit and were horrified to discover that the building plot they had chosen was still just that. No building work had been undertaken at all. They complained to the developer's agent, to no avail, and had to wait two years for their villa to be completed. Their contract stated that compensation would be paid if the building programme extended over three months from the estimated completion date, but they were never offered this and to seek compensation would have involved them in an expensive legal battle.

Other things that can go wrong with a development are:

- The urbanization is illegal.
- Unpaid taxes.
- Unregistered title deeds – *escritura*.
- Difficulty in obtaining municipal services.
- No planning permission.

TIP

When purchasing in Spain it is important that your Spanish legal representative checks that there are no debts related to the property. In Spanish law, you will be responsible for these debts.

UNDERSTANDING THE PAPERWORK

Title deeds – *Escritura publica*

The escritura publica is the registered title deed of the property. It is inscribed in the *Registro de la Propiedad*, which is the property registry. This deed is the only rock solid proof of title to land and property in Spain. If your vendor, be it a developer or a private sale, cannot produce their *escritura*, then all may not be what it seems. The title deed contains details of the description and location of the property. If there are any debts, such as mortgages against the property, they will be registered in the margins of the house deeds. It is wise to see the title deeds, if only as proof that the vendor actually owns the property. If your vendor is unable to supply you with this deed and you are determined to purchase, you could ask for a *Nota Simple*.

Nota simple

This can be obtained by your lawyer from the Registry and contains the relevant details and any mortgages against the property. You can also access this on the Internet, if you are entered in the Registry. It is always preferable, however, to see the *escritura publica*, if this is possible.

TIP

Make sure the *escritura* mentions the property you have purchased, as well as the land it stands on, as sometimes this important detail can be omitted!

Purchasing a property without an *escritura*

It is not uncommon that property in Spain can change hands several times, without anyone actually having the *escritura*. In the UK, the house deeds become yours on completion, but in Spain it can take several months, if not years, to obtain the house deeds. This practice makes me nervous and I would again advise caution when the *escritura* is not readily available, or at least available within an agreed legal timeframe.

Whilst researching this chapter in Spain and talking to several Spanish property owners, I only met one British couple who actually had their *escritura* – the others were still waiting, for one reason or another! Some of the reasons can be:

◆ For the developer to avoid the payment of transfer taxes and fees, which can total 10% or even more of the value.

◆ The owner may want to conceal assets from a creditor, tax collector or spouse.

◆ The property has never been declared to the tax authorities (if previously owned).

◆ There is a dispute with the developer.

IBI receipt – municipal real estate tax

This mainly concerns second-hand properties. When purchasing a second-hand property, you must always ask to see the paid up receipt for the *IBI* before signing any contract, otherwise you may find yourself liable for back taxes or penalties. The *IBI* will show the officially assessed value of the property and this will be what the relevant taxes will be based on. Generally the assessed value of a property will be considerably less than the market value. The *IBI* is the tax set by the local authority and is similar to the council tax system operating in the UK. If the *IBI* payment is late, a 20% surcharge can be added. If you are not resident in Spain and in order to avoid forgetting payment, you can arrange for this charge to be debited from your account.

Referencia catastro

This is a reference number and every property must have one. It will be noted on the *IBI* receipt. This reference will contain all the details relating to the property, including boundaries, property description and location. If there are any major discrepancies between the particulars you have been given by the estate agent and the *catastro*, then you can assume that something may be wrong. Without the *catastro*, you will not officially know the true boundaries of your property and this could involve problems further down the line, should you choose to sell. It is always better to be safe than sorry, no matter what the estate agent may say! If you want to see relevant documentation relating to your purchase, don't be put off, even if it is inconvenient for the vendor or the vendor's agent.

TIP

A new property purchased from a developer will not have an *IBI* receipt yet. It will be your responsibility to register the property for this tax. Make sure your developer has made a declaration of a new building and has paid the small registration tax associated with this.

Community fees/receipts

These are the fees that you will be responsible for if you buy an apartment, townhouse, villa or property in an urbanization area. They are similar to service charges in the UK. They will include upkeep of such things as:

◆ communal gardens
◆ pools
◆ lifts
◆ reception areas.

In an urbanization they will include:

◆ roads
◆ lighting
◆ communal areas.

The receipt for any community fees paid will give you an indication of how much your monthly charges may be. It is also advisable to see the minutes from any meetings relating to these charges, as they will highlight any difficulties you may encounter when purchasing the property.

TIP

As in the UK, a well-run development, with low service charges and a good management company, will only enhance the value of your property. Equally, high service charges and a badly run development will have a negative effect on your property.

Town urban plan

If you want to make sure that no new road is planned at the bottom of your Spanish garden, ask your lawyer to check the *Plan General de Ordenacion Urbana*.

If you are purchasing in Spain from a non-resident

If you are purchasing from a non-resident in Spain, you will have to pay a 5% deposit to the authorities, in the vendor's name, as a guarantee that they will pay their taxes. You will need a Form 211 to justify your payment and you will have to show this to the notary, as proof that you have made this payment. This payment serves as a guarantee against the non-resident's Spanish capital gains tax liability and the 5% will be deductible from the purchase price.

CHECKLIST

Before signing anything, or handing over any money, there are certain guidelines you should try to follow.

- Get advice from a Spanish lawyer.
- Ask to see
  - the *escritura*
  - the *nota simple*.
- the *IBI* receipt
- the *catastro* certificate.
- paid up receipts for community fees
- paid up receipts for all utility bills.
- Get a translation of the contract into your own language.
- Agree your form of payment.
- Pay fees and taxes and the 5% deposit, if buying from a non-resident.
- Ask for confirmation of when you will get your final *escritura*.

Other costs you may incur

I spoke to one British investor in Spain who told me that investing in an off plan Spanish property is like a dripping tap – once you have paid the initial deposit, there is a constant drip to pay more. Extras included items such as:

◆ white goods
◆ water heaters
◆ central heating
◆ terracing
◆ swimming pool
◆ paying for the *escritura*.

TIP

When choosing your Spanish property, flush out what those hidden extras will cost. Developer's agents are quite happy to show you a villa with all the 'trimmings', without fully explaining what is **not** included. You may end up being unpleasantly surprised if you do not fully ascertain exactly what is included in the purchase price!

OTHER CONSIDERATIONS

The villa itself
Surprise, surprise – villas in Spain can actually be very cold inside, even when it is warm outside. They are not built like British houses and have little insulation. If you are thinking about spending a lot of time in your property during the off-peak season, consider the central heating factor. Although such a system will be expensive to install, it may well prove to be economical in the end, particularly if you later come to rely on electric heaters. Electricity in Spain is expensive, as it has to come from France. Another alternative would be to install a solar heating system.

The terrace
When you are shown your villa, make sure the landscaping of the villa is included. This will involve levelling the land and tiling

around the terrace and the pool area. If it is not included, make sure you get an estimate for the cost, as it can be very expensive. In many urbanizations where this is not included, you could end up with endless villas sitting in sandy dust bowls, where DIY chaos abounds. I visited a development recently, where the majority of the villas were not sitting in pretty tiled terraced gardens but in messy building plots. Some of them had been like that for years!

Big developments
Make sure you know how big the urbanization intends to spread. You could end up living in a glorified building site for ten years. This will mean living with constant building dust and noise.

Re-sales
If you invest correctly, you can still make money on the Spanish property market, but don't forget you will be subject to capital gains tax. The non-resident's capital gains tax is 35% of the profit. As of December 31st 1996, Spain ended their tax exemption for property owners of over ten years, and introduced an inflation correction factor. Even with this, the capital gains tax bill will still be considerable and you will have to factor this in when calculating your profits. Another cost factor to consider is estate agents' fees, which are more substantial than in the UK and range from 5% to 10%.

Income tax
Non-resident owners of Spanish property are required, by law, to declare 2% of the official rated value of the property as if it were income. They must pay tax on this income and as non-residents their income tax rate is 25%.

Getting there

Easy Jet and Ryanair offer cheap flights. How long these flights will remain cheap is something to consider. You will also pay more for flights during peak holiday times. The approximate journey time to Spain is two hours flying time. Do not forget to calculate into your travel time how long it will take you to travel from the airport to your Spanish destination. If it is a long distance from the airport, this could affect the desirability of your property from a re-sale or rental point of view.

Time zone

Spain is one hour ahead of GMT.

The Golden Mile

The most prestigious area on the Costa Del Sol is between Marbella and Puerto Banus. One of the new up and coming areas is situated between Estepona and Marbella, although some experts think that this area is now becoming over-priced and over-developed. Obviously you will need to consider this, if you choose to buy.

The golf factor

Golf is emerging as a massive attraction in Spain. There are golf courses sprouting up all over the country. If your property is not situated on the coast, its proximity to a golf course will greatly increase your 'property profit potential' and will also add to the property's appeal with regard to the rental market.

Currency, tourist board and consulates

The currency is the euro and tourist information can be obtained from www.spain.info. The British Consulate can be found at Plaza Calvo Sotelo, 1–2/1o, Alicante, tel: 96 521 6022. The Irish

Consulate is at Gran Via Carlos 111, 94 10o, 2a Barcelona, tel: 93 491 5021.

Average daytime temperatures

- January/February 15°–16°
- March /April 18°–20°
- May/June 22°–24°
- July/August 28°–30°
- September/October 25°–30°
- November/December 15°–18°

SUMMARY

Yes, you can still make money in this buoyant property market, but be careful. If you follow the advice in this chapter and shop around to find the best developments, in the best areas, with the best builders, you could be onto a winner. But if you rush in, without thinking, having had too much sun and Sangria ... you could get burned!

Other Foreign Markets

I think the investment opportunities that are springing up overseas are exciting opportunities, not only to make money but also to have some fun as well. The golden rule applies, however. No matter how tempting it is to buy your dream home in the sun, make sure you do your homework – after all it's your precious money that you are playing with. Always be safe rather than sorry. That doesn't mean to say you can't take risks, just make sure they are calculated ones!

INVESTING IN DUBAI

It's impossible to ignore the fact that Dubai has now emerged onto the property scene. In the next five years the city-state of Dubai will become one of the largest construction sites in the Middle East. There are plans to build the largest skyscraper in the world, the Burj Dubai, along with golf courses, hotels, apartment blocks, water-parks, cinemas, sports complexes and marinas. Dubai is the only place in the Gulf where freehold property can be purchased. By 2008 it is predicted that there will be 200 new skyscrapers and 250,000 new homes built in Dubai. Once famous for its pearls, Dubai is now emerging as one of the fastest growing tourist destinations in the world.

The man behind the plan

Sheikh Mohammed bin Rashid Al Maktoum is the Crown Prince of Dubai. Just under two years ago, he opened the gates for foreign nationals to purchase freehold property in Dubai, making it the only region in the Gulf where property can be owned by westerners. Oil, which was discovered in the Arab emirates in 1966, is expected to run out in the next 20 years and Sheik Mohammed has decided to re-invent the country as a leading tourist resort. Last year 3.5 million tourists chose to holiday in Dubai, and out of this number 300,000 were from the UK. This number is expected to rise by 20% over the next few years.

Shortage of beachfront

Dubai has a shortage of beachfront and, in order to circumvent this problem, man-made islands in the shape of palm trees are being built, which will extend beachfront property. The current availability of 60 kilometres will be expanded to over 200 or more kilometres of seafront real estate. The Palm Jumeirah is currently beginning to emerge from the Gulf and scheduled for completion in 2005, with its sister island, the Palm Jebel Ali (not yet visible), scheduled for completion in 2006/7. The construction of the two Palms to ground level will cost in the region of £2billion per Palm. The plans for each of these man-made islands include 2,400 proposed shoreline apartments and villas, 40 hotels, marinas, restaurants and cinemas. There are further plans to build yet more artificial islands in the shape of the globe.

Dubai: Key facts

- Part of the United Arab Emirates.
- GDP: £1 trillion.
- Over one million additional people will be living and working in the Jumeirah, Umm Suqeim and Jebel Ali districts by 2010.
- Literacy rate is 78%.
- Passenger traffic through Dubai Airport rose by 18% to 16 million last year.
- Key industries: international trade, manufacturing, finance,

tourism and property. The four 'free zones' – Jebel Ali, Dubai Airport, Dubai Internet City and Dubai Media City – are home to more than 3,000 companies.

◆ Oil and gas form 10% of GDP.

◆ GDP growth rate: 2.4%.

◆ Currency: the UAE dirham is fixed to the US dollar, so property prices fluctuate with the pound-dollar rate.

◆ Mortgages: from major banks including HSBC, with interest rates linked to the UK.

◆ Visas and residency are issued to new owners and immediate family. They can be renewed every three years for a fee. The owner must visit Dubai at least once every six months to continue to qualify for residency.

◆ Climate: October to June is warm to hot with little rainfall. The temperature in the summer months can reach an uncomfortable 50°C.

◆ Languages: Arabic and English.

◆ Flights: BA or Emirates, seven hours from London. Also flights from Birmingham and Manchester.

◆ Population: 1 million and continuing to rise. 30% Dubai nationals, 30% Europeans and 40% from the subcontinent.

◆ All properties can be rented or re-sold. There are no local taxes to pay when you buy or sell, although you may be liable for taxes in the UK on rental income or proceeds of sale.

◆ Alcohol is permitted.

◆ Western dress is acceptable for women.

◆ Major developers are Nakheel (government owned), see www.thepalm.ae; Damac, see www.damacproperties.com; Emaar, see www.emaar.com.

Overview

Dubai offers some of the best value in terms of specification and square footage in the overseas property market. Build quality is good, apartments are spacious and all developments come with free gyms and swimming pools. Petrol is cheap and the economy is stable. In fact the future looks positively rosy for the property investor to buy in Dubai. However no one can predict future rental yields and re-sale values, as the extent of the new build programme is vast and the tourist trade is still in its infancy.

Shopping is limited, the weather is unbearably hot during the peak summer months and Dubai has little to offer (as yet) in the way of culture. It is also hardly on the doorstep, making a quick hop for a weekend in the sun unviable. Another drawback could be regime change. If the Crown Prince is removed from power, then the new laws that he has pushed through allowing non-nationals to purchase freehold property could be revoked and westerners may find themselves ousted from their properties with no compensation. It's a gamble, but the pickings could be rich for those brave enough to purchase early in a good development in the right location. I'm tempted ... are you?

INVESTING IN FLORIDA
Florida is known as the sunshine state and its good climate attracts visitors all year round. The include not just the Disney enthusiasts but also golfers, scuba divers, fishermen, tennis players and sailors. There has been a big swing in purchasing property from Europe to Florida, purely on the basis of the favourable exchange rate. The UK, where scarcity of land drives up prices, is different from the US, where a lot of land is available. This is reflected in the property prices and goes some way to explaining why British investors get so much more for their pound than they do at home. Capital appreciation is currently running at a respectable 10% per annum in the Orlando region.

The holiday homes available can range from self-contained villas to condominiums with shared facilities. Villas with four bedrooms, air-conditioning, pool and located within a 15 minute drive from Disney World, offer fairly secure rental possibilities during the peak season, but it is important to check whether short-term lets are permitted, before you purchase.

Long-term lets

As well as short-term holiday lets, Florida can be a good long-term rental investment as well. Properties further away from Orlando, edging towards Florida's Gulf Coast, are cheaper and can provide good rental opportunities for those not necessarily interested in the faster pace of life associated with Orlando. The combination of lower capital costs, fewer void periods and less competition can produce a higher rental yield. The property may not necessarily have to be furnished. Other running costs, such as heating and electricity, will be covered by the tenant, unlike short-term lets where the utility costs are included in the rental. It is really a question of what you are hoping to achieve from your investment: a holiday home, which helps finance itself, or an investment property for long-term lets and higher rental yields.

Rental market overview

Fewer US citizens are travelling abroad since 9/11 and many are now taking holidays in Florida. As in the UK, if a holiday home is in the right location, correctly priced, it will rent out easily during the peak season. There are currently over 12,000 holiday homes for rental close to the Disney area, but demand falls rapidly for short-term lets the further away your property is located.

The higher standard of specification offered will be an important consideration when aiming to maximise on rental opportunities. Florida is a family market and properties that offer four bedrooms can accommodate two families sharing. When calculating any income from rental, it would be prudent to consider the letting season as lasting 30–35 weeks, anything else would be optimistic. If you are in any doubt about projected rental figures, consult an accountant or tax consultant who is familiar with the local market, before falling for any estate agent or developer's hyped up figures.

Sterling mortgages

A sterling mortgage will enable you to calculate your outgoings for the term of the mortgage. This will be useful if you are hoping to invest in a property that you will be using yourself, as well as renting out as a holiday let. It will allow you to match income to expenditure in a single currency. It will also save you having to make dollar transactions at exchange rates which could vary during the lifetime of the mortgage. Most Florida based mortgage companies, with satellite offices in the UK, can offer 80% of the value of the property. Self-certified mortgages are also available at 75%, with no proof of income required. Sterling mortgages are currently being offered at 1.7% above the Bank of England base rate.

Dollar mortgages

Interest only mortgages are available from some US based companies, currently at 1.95% per year. There are also fixed rate mortgages available, which track the US bond rate. A typical repayment mortgage is currently at around 3%. The sterling/dollar exchange rates, although favourable now, could change in the future, so bear this in mind if you intend to gear yourself highly.

Purchase costs

The 'closing' costs are similar to those in the UK and you should allow 3% to 5% of the purchase price to cover costs and disbursements. Furniture will also be an expense that you will have to factor in. As properties tend to be larger in Florida than in the UK, you should overestimate rather than underestimate this particular expense. Some developers of new build properties offer furniture packs and this may be something you will want to take advantage of, if you are UK based.

Property management

If you live in the UK, there is no getting away from the fact that Florida is a long way from home. You will need to employ the services of a professional letting agent, one who offers a comprehensive management service. If you choose to let out the property yourself, you will need to advertise it on the Internet. However, there is nothing to stop you doing both, if you want to maximise rental opportunities.

If you are purchasing a self-contained villa for rental, there will be a lot of maintenance issues that you will need to consider, such as the upkeep of the pool, pest control, gardening, house cleaning and payment of utility bills. A specified agent will take care of these for you, the cost of which will have to be factored into your overall budget. An agent will also advise on local licensing and fire regulations.

Zoning regulations

If you intend to rent out your property, make sure that you are in an area which is zoned for rental. Some zones allow short-term rentals, while others require that the property be let for a

minimum period of four weeks. Some can insist on a minimum of
six months.

Rental schemes
Some rental guarantee schemes may not be as good, in reality, as
they appear on paper. Always make sure that you research any
such schemes thoroughly.

Visas
As a UK citizen, you will be restricted to a 90 day stay in the US
without a visa. If you have a visa, you will be restricted to a
maximum of a six month stay in any given year. Other restrictions
may apply, so make sure you check this out before deciding to
purchase.

Professional advice
You need to be represented by a broker or an estate agent. Your
broker should be a member of the Florida Real Estate Commission
and also of the Multiple Listings Service (MLS). Your agent should
be able to provide you with information on the local community
and comparative data on property prices in the area.

Useful websites
Florida Tourist Guide: www.flausa.com
Informative website: www.escape2.com or www.escape2.usa.co.uk

INVESTING IN CROATIA
The Republic of Croatia is a European country situated along the
Adriatic Sea and its hinterland. It stretches from the slopes of the
Alps and deep into the Pannonian Valley, to the banks of the
Danube and the Drava rivers. Prior to the civil war in Yugoslavia
in the early nineties, over 800,000 foreign tourists had visited

Dubrovnik alone, including myself, and I have to say that I was very impressed by the beauty of the old town and the golden coast of Dalmatia.

When my children were younger, during the civil war between the Croats and the Serbs, I had an au-pair from Croatia who lived with us for two years. She would show me photographs of her beautiful country and speak of its wonderful climate. My Croatian au-pair has long since gone back home and Croatia is now being hailed as possibly the next big thing in the tourist hot spot list.

New developments

Croatia has a long way to go before it catches up with Spain (if it ever does) and the prices reflect this. The quality of some of the new developments is questionable and there are few to choose from. No one could accuse Croatia (yet) of being overdeveloped like the Costas. The better bargains can be found in rural Croatia, where there are farmhouses and buildings in need of repair, or plots of land which are available for sale.

Key facts

- Population: 4.4 million.
- Currency: kuna.
- Croatia was founded on the ruins of the Roman Empire.
- Climate: Mediterranean and continental. Hot summers and cold winters.
- Zagreb is the capital city of Croatia and is the country's political, economic, intellectual and cultural centre.
- Istria is the most developed Croatian tourist region and is most easily accessible from Western Europe. Vineyards and picturesque little towns are scattered all over the interior of the peninsula.

- Dalmatia is a region of long beaches and ancient towns, such as Zadar, Sibenik, Split, Trogir, Omis and Dubrovnik.
- Split is the second largest city in Croatia and the regional capital of Dalmatia.
- Dubrovnik, a medieval aristocratic republic from the 12th–19th centuries, is the best preserved walled city in the Mediterranean and a world heritage site.
- Korcula is an island and is the birthplace of Marco Polo.
- Croatia has seven national parks.
- The economy emerged from its mild recession in 2000, with tourism the main factor.
- Massive unemployment remains a key negative element.
- Croatia is prone to destructive earthquakes.
- Current issues: landmine removal and reconstruction of infrastructure, as a consequence of the 1992–1995 civil war.
- Literacy rate: 98.5%.
- Language: Croatian 96%, others 4%.
- Industries: manufacturing, shipbuilding, petroleum refining, textiles, paper, wood products, tourism.

Overview

Parliamentarians are far from ratifying the Croatia-Slovenia land and maritime agreement. Serbia and Montenegro are still unable to come to an agreement on the economic aspects of the new Federal Union. Croatia and Italy still continue to debate bilateral property and ethnic minority issues, stemming from border changes after the Second World War. Although to all intents and purposes the conflict in Croatia is over, there are still issues to be resolved. This is not to say that Croatia is not on course to become a popular tourist destination. Properties are cheap and the country is beautiful. Investment opportunities are to be had but you would be wise to research the region you are considering investing in carefully before deciding to purchase.

INVESTING IN THE EUROPEAN UNION

The EU has expanded to include, amongst others, the 'Eastern Eight' – the Czech Republic, Hungary, Poland, Estonia, Lithuania, Latvia, Slovakia and Slovenia. When Spain and Ireland joined the EU, both these countries received significant financial investment to trigger economic growth and new jobs for up to eight years after membership was granted. Similarly these new EU countries can expect an economic boost from increased trade and inward investment, if Spain and Ireland are anything to go by. Which country you choose to invest in, however, will be a decision that you will need to investigate carefully. The general advice is to stick with the larger East European capitals, where west European and American companies already have an established presence and the market economy is relatively mature.

DO'S AND DON'TS OF BUYING OVERSEAS

♦ Do check that you will be able to get a mortgage. Most mortgages, particularly in Europe, assess your ability to borrow from your net income. A maximum 35% of income should cover existing outgoings, including your UK mortgage and your proposed euro loan.

♦ Don't rely on rental income to cover all the property outgoings. Always consult local specialists and UK holiday companies for a realistic rental valuation.

♦ Do be aware of any tax implications relating to the property.

♦ Don't sign anything until you have consulted your lawyer.

♦ Do remember that inheritance tax laws can differ from those in the UK and make sure you aware of what these differences are.

◆ Don't hand over any money until instructed by your legal advisor.

◆ Do ask to see an up-to-date entry of the property at the local land registry.

◆ Don't leave your brains at the airport; be as vigilant about buying a property overseas as you would be in the UK, and if anything ... more so.

◆ Do ask if you will be allowed to make any structural alterations to the property, if you so wish.

◆ Don't expect the property to be automatically connected to utilities. If the property isn't connected, find out how much the connection charge will be.

◆ Do check that the contract guarantees vacant possession on the completion date.

◆ Don't accept the contract price if it isn't a fixed one.

SUMMARY

Buying a property overseas is big business and today the investor is spoilt for choice, with the expansion of the EU and the attraction of long haul destinations, such as Florida and Dubai. Where you choose to invest could be governed by any number of things, such as culture, lifestyle, whether the property is purely for investment or for personal use. One thing is common to all overseas purchases, however, you need to have sound advice in order to purchase your property legally and safely. Another consideration is to minimise your exposure to unfavourable exchange rate fluctuations, as much as you can.

Renovation and Interior Design

I have renovated two houses and one apartment, and I wish I could say that it had all been stress free and that I hadn't been ripped off. I can't say either of those things. Good builders that you can trust are hard to find. I'm not saying that your builder has to be your best buddy but he should be treated like a friend rather than an enemy. It is important to enjoy a good relationship with your builder as it will help make the building work go through much smoother. That's not to say you can't still get stung because you can, but it lessens the odds.

FIRST STEPS

If you are considering refurbishing a property, you may need to obtain planning consents before any work can be undertaken.

Planning permission

If you are replacing 'like with like', such as a new conservatory which is equal in size to the old one, planning permission needn't be sought. If you are considering building an extension that is in excess of 40 cubic metres, you may well need planning permission. If you build anything without planning permission, you could be served with an enforcement order from the Local Planning Office. They will make you take it down, or force you to rebuild it within existing planning consents. If you build an extension or anything similar without planning permission, you could have a problem selling the property as the purchaser's solicitor will want to see copies of planning consents.

You can buy a copy of the 'local plan' from your Local Planning Office. This will give you an idea what their policy is regarding planning issues. I recently applied for an off-street parking facility and this was turned down because it did not fit the local plan for the area. If I had known this beforehand, it could have saved me from launching an expensive appeal!

Conservation areas

If your house is in a conservation area you will need planning consent before you can alter anything externally. The aim of a conservation area is to 'conserve' anything that could be considered of architectural significance. I live in a conservation area and I am baffled about what they are trying to conserve. The local planners are quite arbitrary in their decision making about what is acceptable and what isn't. I have recently watched a whole building being systematically gutted directly opposite me, yet while living in the same style house I am unable to replace my front wall because it is deemed to be of architectural significance. Conservationists will differ in their opinions and there are no hard and fast rules. It could just be a matter of who gets to decide your case on the day, whether they will be sympathetic to your requests or not. I obviously caught one on a bad day!

Building regulations

There are two levels of building regulation requirements and both applications are obtainable from you Local Planning Office.

♦ **Building notice**. This is only required for minor works such as the relocation of a bathroom or kitchen. This will involve a site visit by the building inspector to check that the correct regulations are being followed.

♦ **Full plans application**. This will involve sending copies of the working plans to the building inspector for their approval. They will consider all aspects of the proposed plans and whether they comply with fire regulations.

♦ In a **leasehold** property check that the freeholder will grant permission before you undertake any changes.

TIP

If you are planning to purchase and refurbish a leasehold property, check the lease before you purchase, to see whether any restrictions are imposed regarding the alterations you may wish to make to the property.

WHAT ARE YOU RENOVATING THE PROPERTY FOR?

If you are going to renovate a property, you will need to consider what you are renovating it for. Is it to live in, sell on or renovate for rental? Once you have made this decision, you will have to think about your budget and how much you want to spend, as each category will require a different spending plan.

Renovating the property to live in yourself

If you are choosing to live in the property, you may not want to, or be able to afford to do all the renovation work at the same time. As you are not doing the renovation for immediate profit, this shouldn't be a problem nor should the time scale. It will be directly governed by you. What gets done when and in which order of priority is up to you.

TIP

If your property needs a total renovation and is for the most part uninhabitable, you may not want to live in the property while the work takes place, so this could be an expense that you need to factor in. If you have to live in the house, you will need to get certain rooms done first, in order to make life easier for yourself. The most important room to get in place will be the kitchen, as this is the beating heart of most households. You will, of course, need to have a bathroom that is workable!

Renovating to sell on

If you are renovating the property for a quick turnaround profit, your budget will be tighter, as you will have to pay for all the work to be done in double quick time. The sooner the property is complete, the sooner you will be able to market it, so that the mortgage repayments don't cut into your profit too much. Any mortgage repayments need to be included in the budget for renovation, as do legal costs and stamp duty. Whatever costs you incur will come out of your anticipated profit, so it is advisable to keep costs low when doing a 'sell on' renovation. The properties that are best for renovation are the lower to middle range end of the market, as these will not require expensive high tech appliances.

Renovating to sell on to the higher end of the market

If you are renovating a property to appeal to the higher end of the market, this will make your initial outlay that much greater. You will have to think about state of the art kitchens, granite or stainless steel work surfaces, limestone bathrooms, marble tiles, real wood floors, high quality appliances and energy efficient heating systems, to name but a few. These things do not come cheap and will probably increase the amount you have to borrow in order to complete the works. This in turn will increase the mortgage interest that you will have to pay out until the property is sold. Which in turn will decrease your 'property profit potential' if your property is too expensive for the majority of buyers and is sitting on the market for some time, waiting for a purchaser.

TIP

If you are thinking of renovating a property for re-sale, don't be over ambitious with your first property. Aim for a small family house or apartment. It is possible to make a property look good (as long as it is structurally sound) with flair and imagination. You do not need to throw bucketfuls of money at it to get that designer touch.

Renting out your property after renovation

This will affect your budget choices. You will not want to put in high specification appliances and fancy finishes. You will want the renovation to be based on practical and durable lines, with furniture and décor that can stand up to wear and tear.

SURVEYS

Before you commit to purchasing any type of property for renovation, you will need to have a survey done. You will not be able to get a mortgage offer without one and if you are buying the property outright, you will still need a survey to evaluate what works are necessary.

There are three types of survey:

◆ **A basic valuation**. This is a condition of any mortgage being offered by the lender. The cost of the valuation has to be met by the borrower but is for the benefit of the lender. A basic valuation will look at the structure of the house and any other issues that could affect the property's value. The surveyor will also value the property and the building society or bank will offer you a mortgage based on that valuation. The cost of the valuation report will depend on the size and value of the house.

◆ **A homebuyer's survey.** This can be done at the same time as the basic valuation. It will work out cheaper for the borrower if both are done together. A 'homebuyer's survey' is for the benefit of the borrower and is much more detailed than the basic valuation. It will look at the general décor of the property, as well as looking for any defects. It is not foolproof, however, as surveyors tend to survey only what they can see. They will not lift carpets, look under floorboards or scramble around on roofs. If they suspect a specific problem such as damp, they might advise you to get a specialist in to investigate. As this survey is for your use, you will have to foot the bill. Your surveyor will, however, be accountable to you, should they miss something that they should have investigated.

◆ **A full structural survey.** This is a comprehensive survey that is done by a fully qualified chartered surveyor. It is generally only necessary for properties that are in any way unusual or older properties, where there may be a considerable amount of refurbishment to be done. This is a detailed survey for the benefit of the borrower only and will be quite expensive, as the surveyor will have to write you a fully comprehensive report. Specialist help may be recommended.

Case study
I once asked a surveyor to look at two specific aspects of a property: the roof supports and for any evidence of subsidence. The surveyor failed to spot that 17 of the roof supports were ▶

infected with dry rot. We tried for legal recourse against the surveyor but he wriggled out of it, using the excuse that the affected areas were not visible at the time of his inspection. As a consequence of this we had to do remedial work for dry rot, which was expensive and unpleasant, as part of the roof had to come off. Since then I have always liked to take the advice of a builder, as well as a surveyor ... just to be on the safe side!

A COSMETIC REFURBISHMENT

As long as the property is structurally sound and the roof is not caving in, it may be possible to change the whole look of a property without calling in an army of tradesmen. A cosmetic refurbishment is not an excuse, however, to paper over the cracks. If the property is damp, for instance, the problem will have to be sourced and eradicated, otherwise doing any kind of internal decoration will be a waste of time and money. A cosmetic refurbishment is generally done on a house that is basically in good repair but is dated and in need of modernisation and a general overhaul. This kind of house can be suitable for all three categories of renovation, to live in, to sell on or to rent out, but is particularly geared towards a rental investment.

TIP

If the property is to be revalued after a cosmetic refurbishment and, assuming the rental figures stack up, you may be able to remortgage the property – if it is valued higher after the cosmetic refurbishment than it was when you purchased it. You may be able to release this equity from the property and re-invest it to do a cosmetic refurbishment on another house. A lot of landlords increase their property portfolio this way.

KITCHENS

Kitchens are an important part of any refurbishment plan, be it a cosmetic makeover or a total redesign. A kitchen does not need all the mod cons to make it look good. It helps, but if the budget can't run to it, then there are other ways to spruce up a kitchen.

- **Cupboard doors** can be painted. If you paint the doors in an eggshell based paint they can easily be wiped down. Paint them in pale colours so as not to dominate the kitchen.

- Change the **handles** on the units for something more contemporary.

- If the **work surfaces** are past their sell by date, they will have to be replaced. Granite is hard wearing but an expensive option if you are developing a property to make the maximum profit. There are cheaper options made out of laminate, which are practical and durable.

- The **cooker** will have to be in reasonable condition. Quite often, all a tatty looking cooker needs is a good clean, but if you do clean it within an inch of its life and it still looks shoddy, you will have to replace it.

- Paint the **walls** a light fresh colour, as this helps give the kitchen a clean image.

- If there is a window in the kitchen put in a **blind**. This will help give the kitchen a cleaner line.

- If the **floor** is marked and shoddy looking, replacing it with some linoleum is an economical option. There is a vast range to choose from, but again go for something neutral and understated. You do not want to inflict your taste onto a potential buyer.

♦ A few brightly coloured **pictures** can add a touch of colour but can also be removed easily.

♦ A brightly coloured **tea towel**, in a strategic place, can add that designer touch.

♦ **Flowers** – if they're fake, make them sunflowers. If they're real, you'll have to keep replacing them.

TIP

When presenting a property, for either sale or rental, think of adding small things that will enhance its look, rather than large things which will overwhelm it. Good fake fruit in a bowl adds a touch of colour (don't use real fruit unless you are there to replace it regularly) and adds that creative touch.

BATHROOMS

There are no short cuts where bathrooms are concerned. They have to look presentable, but it is possible to make them look good, without having to replace everything.

♦ If the bath is chipped, it may be possible to re-enamel it, rather than have it replaced.

♦ If the sink looks uninspiring or old fashioned, maybe all it needs is a change of taps.

♦ If the tiles are not cracked and are in reasonable condition, you could always re-grout them, to give them that fresh look.

♦ Put in an attractive mirror.

If you have had to renovate an old bathroom rather than put in a new one because of budget restrictions, then accessorise it by adding colour co-ordinated soap dish, toothbrush holder, bathmats and towels.

Case study
I had to replace a bathroom that was beyond repair and not only needed a new bathroom suite (it was orange!) but also needed to be totally re-plumbed, as there was a lot of lead pipework that needed to be removed. I chose a Corgi registered plumber but came unstuck. I tried to take this matter up with Corgi but they only cover a plumber's work in relation to gas boilers. My plumber had attempted to put in my new bathroom and had bungled it completely. He turned out to be a nightmare and swindled, not only us, but also his colleagues. He disappeared before he could face the music, leaving a trail of destruction in his wake.

Just because a plumber is Corgi registered, doesn't mean that you are necessarily protected. If you don't know a good plumber, see if the local tile shop can recommend anyone. They may know one because they provide tiles for bathrooms and a lot of plumbers do their own tiling work. Alternatively, ask in a bathroom showroom. They may have plumbers that they use regularly and have a successful track record. They may not want to pass on their valuable plumber to you though, so ask nicely.

DECORATING

This is a job that can transform any house. It is the icing on the cake. The slog is done, the surfaces are well prepared and ready for the wallpaper or paint. I prefer to do my own decorating if:

- I've got the time
- the ceilings are not too high
- there's not too much preparation work to do
- the room is not too big and the job is not too vast
- it's not a hall, stairs and landing.

Decorating for re-sale and rental

If you are selling the property on, you will want to keep the decorative finishes neutral. I hate to say it but creams and whites are the best option, as they will allow the purchaser to see the property without someone else's decorative stamp on it. If you paint the walls to the colours of your choice, you may alienate a potential buyer.

Neutral colours also make rooms look bigger, as dark colours close a room in more. What you are trying to sell is the space and therefore it makes common sense to show the space in the most flattering light. Clean, uncluttered rooms not only work well from a re-sale point of view but also from a rental point of view, as any prospective tenant will prefer to live in a well presented 'light' property.

GARDENS

Ignore gardens at your peril. If they look overgrown and unkempt, they will put off buyers. If nothing else, make sure that the lawn is cut, the hedges are looking trimmed and the borders are not overgrown with weeds. If the patio area looks dirty, clean it with a pressure pump. If it still looks dull, cheer it up with some pots of brightly coloured flowers.

TIP

If you are going to rent out a property with a garden, make the garden as low maintenance as possible. Tenants are unlikely to nurture gardens and water plants regularly. If the garden has a lawn, you may want to consider paving it or gravelling it over.

CONSERVATORIES

Conservatories are very fashionable and can add value to a property, as they create extra space. A well designed conservatory can enhance the back of a house and I have seen some stunning conservatories, which have been incorporated into the family kitchen and made an integral part of the house.

TIP

If you are thinking about putting in a conservatory or replacing an existing one, consider installing underfloor heating. This works well in conservatories and affords more wall space, as most of the conservatory will be made out of glass and will not be able to accommodate a radiator.

Case study
I inherited a conservatory which was rotten and needed replacing. I had a few estimates but finally decided on a company that had been recommended to me by a friend. I visited a conservatory that the company had built and was impressed. We agreed a price, when the works would commence ▶

and handed over a cheque. The company assured me they were insured for my deposit, should they default for any reason. What I didn't know was that the company was about to go bust. I lost my deposit and could do nothing to reclaim it, as the conservatory company had defaulted on their insurance payments.

TIP

Always pay companies by credit card. This way you are insured. The company may want money 'up front' to order the parts or materials for the conservatory. Ask the company to provide you with proof that they have placed the order and agree to release more funds according to expenditure. Always ask to see a valid insurance certificate.

When choosing a conservatory company, do thorough research!
Some companies go bankrupt and then immediately set up in a different name. If they have no track record, then be cautious. I was led to believe that my 25% deposit was to purchase materials for the conservatory and was necessary to pay the supplier. It turned out that nothing had been ordered and nothing had been paid out for materials. Make sure the conservatory company that you are considering placing your order with has a good reputation. Ask to speak to other clients, don't necessarily go for the cheaper quote and never sign on the dotted line until you have had time to consider the deal. Remember, some conservatory salesmen are very good at the hard sell. They can take an age measuring up but this can be a ploy to try to make you feel guilty if you don't place an order with them.

TIP

If you do sign, make sure you study the terms and conditions thoroughly, as these should include a 'seven day cooling off period', should you choose to cancel your order within that time.

LOFT CONVERSIONS

Loft conversions are another great way of adding space and increasing the value of a house. I turned a three-bedroom house into a four-bedroom house with an extra bathroom. The same principles apply when choosing a loft conversion company as with a conservatory company – do your research. Most loft companies heavily advertise their work during construction by having building signs outside the house (at the discretion of the owner). Check with the owners that they are happy with the way the work is progressing and that the project is running to schedule. Make sure you get at least three quotes and insist on references from other satisfied customers. Ask to personally speak to other clients, as written references can be faked, verbal references are less likely to be so.

If the company is limited then it must be registered with Companies House. You can ask for information regarding the company and they will provide it for a small fee. This information will tell you how long the company has been operating and who the directors are. If the company has only just been registered it may be because they are genuinely starting out, or it may be a warning sign that they have had to change their company name. If you have any doubts about the validity of a company then don't go with them!

Case study
I was having my loft converted by a good builder and I recommended him to one of my friends. My friend wanted to build a roof extension on a four-storey house. I left my builder in charge of our loft conversion and went off to Ireland for three weeks. I was pregnant at the time and wanted the major work to take place whilst I was away. When I returned home, very little work had been done. My builder had been working on my friend's house. The problem was the builder had become greedy and had taken on too much work. The whole building programme was in chaos and the builder went bust because he couldn't organise his time properly and had taken too much on. The builder failed to pay the plumber and there was a lot of bad feeling all round. No one, not even the builder, benefited from this situation.

BASEMENTS

It is becoming increasingly popular to convert basements into living spaces. This is because it is often a cheaper option than moving house and has the advantage of increasing the value of the property. A basement is treated as an extension, in planning terms, so if it exceeds 40 cubic metres, you will need to apply for planning permission. In most cases this shouldn't be refused, as basements have little or no visual impact.

Conservation areas/Greenbelt

The size of extensions is restricted in these areas and the planning permission granted will affect any future, above ground, extension allowances. So, if you are planning to convert the basement and extend, you may have to compromise on space, as both basement and extension will eat into the 40 cubic metre allowance.

Will it be cost effective?

It will be more expensive than an extension but could increase the value of your house by 20% to 30%, so you should be able to recover your costs when you choose to sell.

Won't it have damp problems?

You will need to have the basement waterproofed and your choice of water proof system should be dictated by the level of the water table in your area, the type of soil and the foundation type. To assess ground water conditions, you will need to hire a competent structural engineer or someone recommended by the British Structural Waterproofing Association (www.bswa.co.uk).

Won't it be dark?

You will need to construct a lightwell, which could mean the excavation of all or part of the front garden. You will need planning permission for this. This is likely to stipulate that the changes necessary to the front part of the house have little impact on the character and appearance of the property. From the rear, however, there will be more flexibility and it may be possible to incorporate your basement design into the overall look of your garden.

What fire precautions will I need to take?

A fire exit either through a window or a door must be provided. If it is through a window then the size and position of the window must be situated within fire regulation conditions – the window must be 1.1 metres above the internal floor level. Further details of fire and building regulations are available at www.odpn.gov.uk.

Will my builder be able to do the work?

Basements require specialist knowledge and it would be prudent to seek a professional company whose expertise is in constructing basements. This may be more expensive in the short term but could save you money on costly repairs in the long term. Basement problems are not instantly apparent and could take a year or so to surface. The NHBC are leaning towards recommending that all basements should be installed and designed by a specialist company.

TIP

Be careful when recommending builders. What works for you may not work for your friends. Builders don't like losing work, so they will probably say yes to your timeframe. You need realistic start dates and realistic completion dates. Always hold a substantial payment back, until final completion. Make sure you are happy with the building work before you make any payment.

SUMMARY

Although there have been some difficult moments during the renovation work I have undertaken, it has also been very rewarding both aesthetically and financially. You really can transform a house and breathe life into it with a few well-made decisions. It will depend how far you want to go with your development, how many features you wish to add and what (most importantly from a property investor's point of view) will be most cost effective. Study other houses in the area to see what home improvements others have done. Look at what is popular and what can help you achieve your maximum 'property profit potential'.

(13)

Self Build

Anyone who has ever had work done to their home, no matter how minimal, will tell you that nothing is without problems. I have had extensive renovation work done, particularly on my own house, and there has always been a problem, no matter how simple the job. The problems have ranged from incomplete deliveries, dodgy builders, weather, absenteeism, late deliveries, mistakes, problems with supplies, companies going into liquidation, lost orders to double-booked workforce. In fact the list is endless.

Very few estimated completion dates turn out to be accurate – most building programmes incur some delay, somewhere along the line. So to start self-building work assuming that everything will be plain sailing would be foolish. Expect the worst and then you'll be surprised when it doesn't turn out to be as bad as you predicted. The result will be worth it in the end, as long as you try to stay within budget and in control!

TIP

Have a 'long stop' date in mind. Large developments have these written into their contracts. Basically it means that although you may estimate to have the building works complete by a certain time, you have another later date in mind, just in case there are any unforeseen reasons why things cannot be finished in time. This will help you not to go over budget, if you arrange your finances to take into account that the long stop date will most likely be the actual completion date. Keep this date to yourself, as you want to motivate your workforce to finish as near to the proposed completion date as possible.

WHY DO PEOPLE CHOSE TO SELF BUILD?

It is cheaper – meaning that your house should be worth more
when it's built, assuming it has come in on budget. Most self-build
homes work out to be 20% to 30% cheaper than if you had
purchased a new house on the same plot. It also means that you
can design the house to your own specification, in a location of
your choice (subject to the usual planning consents, of course). It
means that you can have your dream home – or if you are
choosing to build the property and sell it on, then hopefully a
worthwhile profit.

FINANCING A SELF BUILD

You will need to finance your self-build property and have a
mortgage agreed, in principle. There are specialist lenders that
offer mortgages for homebuilding projects. You will need to refer
to the individual lender for details of their stage payment system
and terms and conditions. Most mortgage companies will release
stage payments in arrears and it is important to discuss what your
financial requirements will be during the building construction
phases. A few mortgage companies will release stage payments in
advance. A mortgage can be anything from 75% to 95% of the
building costs and the land costs, but you will need to have some
form of planning consent before the mortgage company will
release funds on the land.

Using equity in your own home

You may also be able to use the equity in your own home, in
conjunction with any mortgage offer and stage payments offered
by the bank or building society. This could mean that your stage
payments would be coupled with the existing payments on your
home loan, enabling you to stay in your current home until your
new property is built.

You need to make sure that you have sufficient funds during the initial construction period and sufficient cash flow to fund the project between each stage payment. If you are doubtful about your cash flow and have no short-term savings to fall back on, you should consider a self-build mortgage that offers advance stage payments, but even then there could still be a gap between each payment.

Deposit

As with most mortgage offers, you will have to come up with a deposit. This can be from the sale of your own home or from savings.

Reclaiming VAT on new build

If you are constructing a new building, the good news is that you can reclaim the VAT on most materials purchased for the house build. The bad news is that you cannot claim this VAT back until after the house is finished. Contact your local VAT Business Advice Office (see local telephone directory) for claim form and information leaflets.

VAT on conversions

If you are converting an existing property, you can claim for materials and also for the services of plumber, electrician or any other specialist service provider. VAT registered builders must charge the reduced VAT rate of 9% on labour and materials, as you will be able to claim this back after the property is complete. Details are outlined in the leaflet entitled 'VAT refunds for do-it-yourself builders and converters' and is available from your local VAT office.

VAT on listed buildings

Approved alterations on listed buildings can carry a zero VAT rating, provided the work has been granted listed building consent and is not a repair or maintenance job. Details are available from Customs and Excise VAT – Buildings and Construction.

TIP

If you are going it alone, check out what software is available to help you plan your budget strategy. Some can estimate the cost of your building project and manage the process from start to finish. These include new builds, extensions, renovations and conversions from either a small plan or a full working drawing.

The budget

This will be dependent on many factors which you will need to decide on before any construction begins. You will have to decide how big you want your property to be, how many storeys it will have and what will be the internal layout. You should also plan how much of the building project you intend to carry out yourself, as this will have an effect on the overall labour costs.

TIP

As foundations and roof work are two of the most expensive elements in any build, a bungalow will work out almost as expensive as a two-storey house of the same internal floor space.

USING A PROJECT MANAGER

If you are new to the self build game and unless you know a considerable amount about building work, you would be well advised to employ someone to project manage the development for you. This could be the architect who has drawn up the plans.

He or she will already have consulted with you and the local planning office to get the plans approved and, if necessary, modified. It could also be a builder who has knowledge of the local workforce and has undertaken similar projects before.

I have project managed small building works myself and they have turned out well, but if I was planning a big build, I would most definitely employ a professional to project manage the job for me. It may cost more initially but it will save a lot of headaches and in most cases save on the overall cost.

Builders

It will be the project manager's job to deal with the builders. It will also be their responsibility to order the materials and to make sure that they are delivered on site at the required time. The project manager will also have to make sure that everything runs according to schedule. This will involve the orchestration of electricians, plumbers, carpenters and anyone else connected with the build. Their other burden will be to control the budget and make sure that the build doesn't run into extra time.

How do I find a good project manager?

A good builder may not necessarily be a good project manager. If you are considering using a builder, check whether they have done any other similar projects in the past and ask to see their work, if possible. If not, ask for references from previously satisfied clients and ask whether you can speak to them personally to check on the 'job satisfaction' level. If the builder has a lot of unfinished projects on the go, be aware that you could end up being one of those unfinished projects. If the builder's last job fell significantly behind schedule, he may not want you to see it and if he doesn't, take that as a warning sign.

Using an architect as project manager

If you are using an architect, ask to see their portfolio and follow the same procedures as you would with a builder. If you employ the wrong person to project manage, your whole development could be put at risk, as this will have a knock on effect all through the building chain.

Personal recommendation

If you know a good builder, plumber or electrician, they most likely will know other professionals who they will be prepared to recommend. It is possible to source your entire workforce from one skilled professional. If they employ good working practices, it is more than likely that the people they recommend will employ the same high standards. I use my plumber to source my workforce, as his standard of work is high and I have the confidence in him to know that he would not recommend someone for whom he does not have a professional respect for.

TIP

Don't employ someone as your project manager whom you suspect you might not get along with. It is important to have a good relationship with your project manager, as this relationship will most likely be put to the test at some point during the building programme. Sometimes a clash of personalities can put the project at risk as much as an unreliable workforce.

DIY PROJECT MANAGING

If you choose to project manage the build yourself and have the time and knowledge, this will obviously work out cheaper than employing a project manager. It will be your job to make sure that all materials are delivered on time and that the correct contractors and labour are able to get on with their jobs at the allotted time. Not easy!

You will need to have to have a lot of time on your hands and a lot of organisational skills in getting the building programme to run smoothly. You will also need a good plumber, electrician, plasterer, as well as builder. In fact I would have an army of them standing by!

TIP

It will also be important for you to get a good supplier so you can order your building materials at trade prices. If you employing a main contractor, they will have their own preferred suppliers where they will already have a trade account in place.

THE COST OF MATERIALS
This will depend on what type of finish you are trying to achieve.

◆ If you are going for standard materials, this will comply with the specification levels provided by most house builders. It will be more 'off the peg' than custom built.

◆ If you are going for a better finish, this will cost more in the budget but you will get superior kitchen installations, joinery, insulation, sanitary ware and under-floor heating, for example.

◆ If you are going for a top of the range finish, with bespoke kitchens, high performance insulation, under-floor heating, hardwood joinery, designer bathrooms and so on, then expect to pay top of the range prices.

What if I want to use only high-quality building materials?

If you are planning the build using stone, natural slate, thatch, handmade bricks, flint panels, timber and so on, you will have to budget with these extra costs in mind, as they will be considerably more expensive than standard materials.

Ground conditions

The cost of developing a site with unusual ground conditions, such as clay or any kind of contamination, can substantially add to your building costs.

TIP

The ground conditions need to be tested by an engineer, as soon as possible. You will not be able to do a comprehensive budget until the site ground conditions have been assessed. If the ground is sloping, this will also add to your building costs.

GETTING STARTED

Where should I live during the build?

If you have decided to sell your home and release the capital to fund the deposit, you will need somewhere to live. This can be rental accommodation or a mobile home on site, or with long-suffering relatives!

TIP

Do not forget to calculate into your budget the cost of storage for your furniture.

Where do I find a plot?

- The local papers often advertise land for sale.
- Auctions often sell plots of land, so it is worth investigating a

few to find out what is on offer.

◆ Estate agents.

◆ Planning applications (check local papers).

◆ Land databases on the Internet.

◆ Check out your local area. Look out for any wasteland or disused/derelict buildings. If you see anything you are interested in, contact your local planning office to find out what the situation is.

◆ Get a detailed map and walk or cycle around the area of your choice.

TIP

Don't be afraid to knock on people's doors if you see a property that would benefit from a bulldozer. You may get a bunch of fives but is also possible that someone might be ready to sell. 'Discovered' building plots like these will invariably work out cheaper than any you find from a database, as these will already be 'found' and, as such, carry a price premium.

Insurance

Insurance is an essential part of any self build programme. You will not only have to insure your property against damage and theft, you will also have to insure it against personal injury. This means that anyone working on or visiting your development is covered, should there be an accident. The insurance cover can also include any mobile home situated on the site. The insurance should cover:

◆ public liability insurance
◆ employer's liability insurance
◆ contract works insurance
◆ building warranty NHBC or ZURICH.

Other additional costs

There will be many other costs involved with any self build project and it is important that these are all calculated into your budget. If you are in doubt about a price, overestimate rather than underestimate. It is always preferable to have money left over, rather than be caught out because of insufficient funds. Other costs will include:

◆ land costs
◆ legal fees, stamp duty and land tax
◆ topographical survey fees
◆ mortgage fees
◆ design fees
◆ planning application and building regulations fees
◆ structural guarantee and insurance
◆ connection of services such as water, electricity, gas, drainage.
◆ demolition works if applicable
◆ landscaping.

DEALING WITH THE AUTHORITIES

Planning permission

It is good to get this ball rolling as soon as possible, as this can often take a frustratingly long time to get. It is always advisable to employ a professional who is well versed with the peculiarities of the planning department, to guide you through this process and fill in all the necessary applications. This can be a designer, architect or planning consultant.

Building regulations

This will involve sending in an application form with detailed drawings showing site location, service locations and block plan.

You will then be allocated a building control surveyor who will look at your plans in detail. If your application conforms to building regulations, you will be issued an approval notice.

What if my building application is refused?
Unlike a planning application, if your plans are rejected they will not go on record. The reasons for the refusal will be documented and you will be allowed to amend your plans and submit them again, without further expense. If the plans are still refused and you think this is unjustified you will need to seek dispensation from the local council. If that fails, you will have to apply to the Department of the Secretary of State. Your building control surveyor will be able to provide you with the details, if you choose this course of action.

Utilities
Before starting any work on site make sure that you contact the necessary authorities in connection with providing temporary services, such as water and power. If you are employing a project manager, arranging these services will be part of their job. If you are intending to provide a generator and a chemical toilet, this will obviously affect your requirements from the electricity company and the water authority. You will, of course, still need to arrange for running water to be available on site

CHOOSING A DESIGNER OR ARCHITECT
This will be one of the most important elements of your self build project. If you are designing for profit rather than personal use, it is important that you choose a designer with commercial acumen rather than one with a reputation for complex ideas. The things to look out for when making a decision are:

◆ Creative skills, imagination and flair (no amount of qualifications will be able to compensate for these, if they don't come naturally).

◆ The ability to listen to what the client wants and not blind them with science and unnecessary technical talk.

◆ Do you like them? This will be very important, as you will be working a lot together.

◆ Track record. Any reputable designer should be proud of their work and will be only too happy to show and discuss their portfolio with you.

◆ Real experience of designing an individual home, as opposed to a large development or commercial project.

◆ Awareness of current building costs.

◆ A willingness to discuss fees.

◆ An understanding of your specific budget requirements and limitations.

Personal recommendation

If you know someone who has recently had some work done on their house which you like and which has involved the services of an architect, ask if they would recommend them. If all has gone to plan and they are pleased with the outcome then they will be happy to do this. If it has been troublesome, even though the end result looks good, you may want to look elsewhere, as a stressed working relationship may not be the best option. It is important to remember, however, that as with all business relationships, you need to make your own decisions about what works for you.

The local planning office

Although they will not be able to directly recommend someone, they will be able to give you a list of names they have worked with in the past and it should not take Sherlock Holmes to work out which ones they prefer. Alternatively, if there is a recently built property that you admire, you can always ask the planning office to see the drawings relating to that site and they will have the name of the designer/architect on them. This will also be a good way of assessing how the plan was presented to the council and ascertaining how the plans were received by them.

The Designers Association

These are designers in principle, because they have not taken their final examinations that allow them to become chartered, although they can possess much the same skills and talents as fully qualified architects. This type of designer is popular with self builders, as they tend to be cheaper than their fully qualified cousins, although in most cases equally as good.

Trade associations

As with all trade associations, just because they are listed doesn't mean that they are the best, but if you have no other way of sourcing a good designer/architect then they are certainly a place to start from.

- Associated Self Build Architects: www.asba-architects.org
- Royal Institute of British Architects: www.architecture.com
- The Architects Registration Board: www.arb.org.uk
- The British Institute of Architectural Technologists: www.biat.org.uk
- Scottish Architects Network: www.scottisharchitects.org
- Royal Incorporation of Architects in Scotland: www.rias.org.uk

- Royal Society of Architects in Wales: www.architecture-wales.com
- Royal Society of Ulster Architects: www.rsua.org.uk
- Royal Institute of Architects in Ireland: www.riai.ie

The local papers

Some companies advertise in the local press, listing the special services they offer.

The client's contribution

It is important that you are clear about what you want. Where possible, take photographs of houses that you like. Cut out any pictures of properties that interest you from newspapers and magazines. If you want to have a go at drawing a rough plan yourself, then do so. At least this will give the architect or designer an idea of what you are after, even if you are not Michaelangelo!

TIP

Be very clear from the beginning about your budget and stipulate clearly that the construction costs must not exceed that figure, as there is no pot of gold hidden under the floor-boards. Explain that your ceiling price is your final price and that you have no margin for extras.

Be in control

During the construction process you may have to compromise on your original design, for financial or practical reasons. Be flexible about these issues, but if you are not happy about any changes, do not be rushed into any decisions. Take time to explore whether there are other ways to get what you want and if there are not, you must be prepared to compromise – but only compromise if you are sure that you can be happy with it.

DECIDING ON YOUR DESIGN

When you consider designing your own property, decide what market you are designing it for. If it is for profit, you will need to consider this when you are calculating your budget. Your local estate agent should be able to help you with this one, as they will be familiar with what type of properties are most in demand in the area. It will be in their interest to give you the correct information regarding this, as they will be hoping for the instruction to sell the property once it is completed.

Understanding good design principles

Whether you choose to employ a designer or not, it is important that you understand good basic design principles. As more and more people are choosing to work from home, it would be advisable to consider providing 'working space' in your overall design. It is also important that you provide at least two bathrooms, as this is an essential for modern-day living. Other aspects which add value are large rooms, natural light and spacious kitchens.

Expensive design options

If you are designing your property for re-sale, you will not want to add expensive luxuries that will eat into your profit margins. These can include such things as:

- ◆ complex shapes
- ◆ overpriced kitchens
- ◆ small rooms
- ◆ bespoke fittings
- ◆ jacuzzi/sauna.

> **TIP**
>
> It is important that any design ideas do not drive up the cost while reducing the profit, especially if you are designing the property with a re-sale in mind rather than for personal use.

A timber-framed house

A growing trend is to use the timber frame construction method. This build route guarantees a quick construction time up to the point where the property is weather-proofed, which is a great plus in the British climate! It also affords superior insulation, making the property much more energy efficient. The house can also come in kit form, ready to be built on site, from start to finish.

Custom built houses

This is when a company takes over the entire build for you. Obviously, you will have to pay for this service, but it may prove cost effective in the long run and it will most certainly save on the 'grief' associated with self build.

REASONS FOR FAILURE

- Bad design. Designing for personal preference rather than your potential market.
- DIY. If you don't know what you are doing, don't do it. Leave it to the professionals!
- The weather, getting bogged down by rain or snow!
- Getting ripped off because you are inexperienced.
- Bad and over-priced suppliers.
- Tense and stretched working relationships.
- Bad planning.
- Losing control.

SUMMARY

Self build is becoming increasingly popular. Some 10% of all new houses built each year are by self builders. The most crucial aspect of any self build project is not only the planning but also to get the right people in place. If you are deciding to go it alone, make sure you get written agreements from all the tradespeople you employ. Shop around for your supplier and constantly check that the materials on order are to be delivered on time. Late deliveries can play havoc with your building programme, particularly if you have tradespeople booked in who are not able to get on with their job. If you do employ good tradespeople (and hopefully you will) then treat them with respect. Make the experience a positive one for the whole workforce. Stay in control and constantly plan and re-plan, and if the jigsaw just does not fit ... don't be afraid to call in a professional!

14

Property Millionaire Workshops

Been there, done that and got the very expensive T-shirt to prove it. Was it worth it? Yes and no. Yes, I did learn some things but no, it was not worth all that money! I could have just as easily picked up the gist of becoming a property millionaire by putting down a lot less money ... in fact by reading this book!

But property millionaire workshops are not just about investing in property, they are about achieving goals, becoming financially independent and living the high life, while the money rolls in from those oh-so-fruitful buy to let investments. If only!

THE EASY LIFE

If it was that easy wouldn't everyone be at it? Wouldn't we all be overnight property millionaires? I know that, since I started to invest in property, I have had to work very hard just keeping everything ticking over and that is with professionally managed properties. It's not just a question of washing your hands, walking away and having a beach bum lifestyle, while everyone else takes care of everything. Maybe that is what we would like to aspire to but in the beginning it's watching the pounds, it's watching the shillings and it's watching the pence. Being a property investor takes commitment, financial strategy, hard work and patience.

You can, in theory, use your equity, borrow the deposit, use someone else's equity, get a loan on valuation, get someone to guarantee you, buy jointly or have someone gift you the deposit.

All these areas have been covered in this book and are perfectly valid ways of making money. But whilst workshops tend to make it all look so easy – and perhaps to a certain few it will be that easy – this book takes a more cautious view by encouraging the small acorns approach: meaning start off small and grow big. This does not have to take a lifetime and, indeed, getting on with it is encouraged, but I would rather have a manageable portfolio to start off with than one that was running away with me. I want to be in the driving seat and in control of my own destiny, as much as I can. Having said that, I admire the dynamic approach these workshops encourage. The 'go for it' rather than 'wait for it' philosophy.

HIGH RISK STRATEGIES

Property millionaire workshops encourage you to borrow money and that is sound business sense – up to a point. It is when they start to talk about using credit cards to finance deposits that I get a bit nervous. Of course it is perfectly feasible to raise a deposit that way. By having five credit cards that allow you £2,000 credit per card, you've soon got £10,000 and, as most credit cards are interest free for the first six months, you could be on to a winner. But the 'what ifs' are huge. What if you lose your job? What if they call in the credit before the allotted time? What if you are ill? What if ... what if ... what if?

Any debt carries a risk but for me, I like to be insured against the 'what ifs' as much as possible and any property investor should look into the insurance factor very carefully. We would all like the sun to be shining all the time but there are rainy days and property millionaire workshops don't seem to focus too much on the downside. Maybe they are right in that approach but for me, although I can live with the odd sleepless night, permanent insomnia is not something I crave ... not even for a fast buck!

Epilogue

I hope you have enjoyed this book and it has helped you in deciding whether being a property investor is for you. If you have decided that this is the path you want to follow, I hope this book will help you avoid a lot of the problems associated with the 'wet behind the ears' investor. Everyone has to start somewhere and if you are serious about jumping on the bandwagon of property, do remember that research is the key word and the key action. If you want to find out whether something is true, then find it out for yourself. Don't fall for estate agent's hype and don't be led off the path of practical investing by trying to run before you can walk.

Start at the shallow end rather than the deep end and consider each financial step, before you take it, in minute detail. If you are over ambitious in the beginning of your property journey, you could come unstuck. Try it out first by buying one property and if it all works out, suits your lifestyle and fits into your long-term plans, then by all means go ahead and expand, but don't overstretch yourself. Always have some money in your budget for emergencies, be it interest rate hikes, void periods, leaky boilers or bad tenants. Remember, Rome was not built in a day, and a property portfolio needs to be built on sound foundations, rather than get-rich-quick schemes.

Manageability and staying in control are the two basic ingredients in the property pie. Without these the recipe could be disaster but with these two key ingredients in place you can have your pie and eat it!

Index